PATRICK McGRATH

Series Preface

Gothic Authors: Critical Revisions is dedicated to publishing innovative introductory guides to writers of the Gothic. The series explores how new critical approaches and perspectives can help us to recontextualize an author's work in a way that is both accessible and informative. The series publishes work that is of interest to students of all levels and teachers of the literary Gothic and cultural history.

Series Editors

Andrew Smith, University of Glamorgan
Benjamin Fisher, University of Mississippi

Editorial Board

Kent Ljungquist, Worcester Polytechnic Institute, Massachusetts
Richard Fusco, St Joseph's University, Philadelphia
David Punter, University of Bristol
Angela Wright, University of Sheffield
Jerrold E. Hogle, University of Arizona

GOTHIC AUTHORS: CRITICAL REVISIONS

Patrick McGrath

Sue Zlosnik

UNIVERSITY OF WALES PRESS
CARDIFF
2011

www.uwp.co.uk

British Library CIP Data
A catalogue record for this book is available from the British Library.

ISBN 978-0-7083-2375-5 (hardback)
ISBN 978-0-7083-2374-8 (paperback)
e-ISBN 978-0-7083-2376-2

Typeset in Wales by Eira Fenn Gaunt, Cardiff
Printed by CPI Antony Rowe, Chippenham, Wiltshire

In loving memory of my mother,
Elsie Wealleans Peters

Acknowledgements

Without the inspiration of the International Gothic Association and its conferences, this book would never have been written.

I am grateful to Manchester Metropolitan University for giving me a term's relief from Head of Department duties and especially grateful to Berthold Schoene and Ann Holmes who saw the need and made it happen. Thank you to excellent colleagues Mike Bradshaw and Linnie Blake who looked after everything in my absence – and to all the members of the Department of English, without whom life would be much less interesting.

Andrew Smith and Benjamin Fisher, the general editors of this series, deserve a special mention. Special thanks too to Avril Horner, my long-time collaborator, who has been so supportive of this solo enterprise. Most of all, I am, as ever, indebted to my family – my three sons, James, Sam and Tom, and my husband, John – for more than I can say.

Finally, Patrick McGrath himself has taken a keen interest in the project and has been more than willing to answer my questions without attempting in any way to influence what I was writing. Thank you, Patrick.

CONTENTS

Introduction

࿓

'Why are you so weird?' According to Patrick McGrath, this is the question he and David Cronenberg asked each other on the set of *Spider*, the 2002 adaptation of McGrath's novel of the same name.[1] The answer to this question is beyond the scope of this book. The persistence of the 'weird' in McGrath's writing, however, is central to its discussion of his work in relation to the Gothic tradition. In a recent interview following the publication of his most recent novel, *Trauma*, he claimed that he did not want to be labelled as a Gothic writer.[2] However, when a new critical edition of Daphne du Maurier's short stories was published in 2008, recent critical recognition of her Gothic sensibility was marked by the fact that it was McGrath who was invited to write an introduction.[3] In spite of his reluctance, he remains the contemporary literary novelist pre-eminently associated with the Gothic; indeed, one reviewer has suggested that 'he may be the best Gothic novelist ever'.[4] When invited to write an essay on the nature of Gothic for Cristoph Grunenberg's *Gothic* (a glossy compilation of material from different art forms) he entitled it 'Transgression and Decay', suggesting that these are the features that define the Gothic in its representation of what Freud identified as 'the death wish'.[5] Recognizing the political potential of Gothic's transgressive tendency, he acknowledges its 'impulse to identify specific conditions and power relations that foster what we experience as evil', and claims that 'Gothic allows us to manage the nightmares of a world in which control seems increasingly tenuous'.[6]

No longer do scholars identify Gothic as a historically defined novel genre, located at the end of the eighteenth century; instead, they tend to see it as a mode of writing intrinsic in all its variations to the rise of modernity.[7] As Fred Botting points out in his introduction to the English Association's 2001 collection of essays, entitled, problematically it would seem, *The Gothic*: 'These days it seems increasingly difficult to speak of "*the* Gothic" with any assurance.' The term, he goes on to suggest, continues to spread, generating a variety of qualifying adjectives ('postcolonial Gothic' and 'queer Gothic', for example, alongside such historically specific terms as 'Victorian Gothic'). This diffusion continues to '"Gothicize" a host of different sites, from a Gothic imagination to a Gothic nature, from body, desire and unconscious to science and technology'.[8] Transgression inevitably implies boundaries; in Gothic, boundaries are transgressed. More disturbingly, they are often shown to be unstable with monstrosity, horror or terror lurking in their liminal spaces. Such a concern with the permeability of boundaries, it has been suggested, manifests a deep anxiety about the coherence of the modern subject.[9] Indeed, Gothic writers deliberately exploit the fear of the 'Other' encroaching upon the apparent safety of the post-Enlightenment world and the stability of the post-Enlightenment subject in order to achieve their effects.[10]

McGrath's discomfort with the label 'Gothic novelist' raises a number of interesting questions. In contemporary writing, where are the limits of Gothic? How do we now define this mode, and how indeed does a writer like McGrath make and remake Gothic writing? This book examines the evolution of his writing, considering each text in turn while identifying continuing threads and establishing connections with the Gothic tradition in which he initially placed himself. Words, images and themes in the early work find expression of increasing complexity in the later novels. As his career has progressed, there has been a shift of emphasis so that the flamboyant parody of the early work gives way to a more subtle intertextuality in its representation of transgression and decay, themes that continue to inform his work. Richard Davenport-Hines's magisterial and interdisciplinary *Gothic: 400 Years of Excess, Horror,*

Evil and Ruin (1998) makes this judgement on McGrath's work up to that date:

> McGrath is a dandyish stylist who depicts tumult, evil, monstrosity, disease, madness, horror and death with hallucinatory menace. Like many early Goth novelists, his narratives often lead the reader into discoveries of danger within what had seemed safe. He is pitiless about human confusion and sometimes painterly in the way of David Lynch. While McGrath's most relentlessly Gothic work seems frivolous or ephemeral pastiche, he achieves superb effects when the Gothicism is relaxed.[10]

Without acknowledging that the early, more overtly parodic, work is 'frivolous or ephemeral pastiche', this book argues that the change of emphasis in the later works achieves a different kind of Gothicism. Whereas the early work is clearly influenced by a postmodern preoccupation with play and parody, the 1996 novel *Asylum* takes the fiction in a different direction. Adopting some of the conventions of realism while continuing to make use of the unreliable and complicit first-person narrator, it presents a text the surface of which appears to be anti-Gothic but with depths that probe disturbingly the boundary between sanity and madness. In *Martha Peake* (2000), realism and postmodern parodic Gothic are played off against each other in a novel that signals the shift into the twenty-first century and into the narratives of America that constitute the later work.

In a 2001 interview, McGrath identified the novelist John Hawkes as a key formative influence on his work. Asked what his literary references were, he replied:

> They change all the time, depending what I'm thinking about in my work. When I got to New York in 1981, I was just starting to write, and that's when I found Hawkes's work. It was a sort of . . . flash. I thought this is – particularly *Travesty* – this is what the novel should be. Psychologically dark, a tight, elegant structure, deeply disturbing, first person narration, slim.[12]

McGrath seems to have found twentieth-century echoes of Poe in Hawkes's work. He likens *Travesty*'s tale of a speeding car, narrated by its mad driver, who is bent on the destruction of his passengers and himself, to Poe's 'The Cask of Amontillado': in both the reader is trapped in the mind of the narrator and in the book itself.[13] When McGrath co-edited with Bradford Morrow a collection of short stories, *The New Gothic*, in 1991, Hawkes was a contributor. This volume pays tribute in its introduction to Poe for turning the Gothic inward 'to explore extreme states of psychological disturbance'.[14]

Published just over a decade later than *The Literature of Terror*, David Punter's ground-breaking critical work, *The New Gothic* may be regarded as a seminal collection, its appearance coinciding with growing momentum in academic interest in the Gothic.[15] It set out to bring together contemporary short stories that, in the editors' judgement, demonstrated that Gothic had survived in mutated forms and was flourishing in the late twentieth century; their preface acknowledges the 'fascinating' Gothic tradition and offers the reader stories 'no longer shackled by the conventional props of the genre', but nonetheless 'strongly manifest[ing] the [G]othic sensibility'.[16] Almost twenty years later, its list of British and American contributors makes for interesting reading. There are some names that are more associated with experimental fiction: in addition to Hawkes, Martin Amis and Jeanette Winterson are both represented here. There are also those whose reputation has developed as serious literary writers with a Gothic sensibility: Angela Carter, Emma Tennant and Janice Galloway. Then there are those who have enjoyed a growing reputation for popular Gothic writing: Scott Bradfield, for example, and, more famously, Anne Rice, whose vampire novels have enjoyed great commercial success.

McGrath himself does not enjoy the commercial popularity of Anne Rice or her spectacularly successful contemporary exponent of Gothic horror, Stephen King (who wrote an unfilmed screenplay of McGrath's novel *Asylum*).[17] He is also less easy to categorize than some of the other inheritors of the Gothic tradition. Although vampirism figures in his fiction, it is not a central theme, as it is in the work of Rice or other noted writers of the sub-genre, like Poppy Z. Brite. His horror tends to be more insidious and more psychological than King's or that of writers like Clive Barker or Dean Koontz; his terrors are less immediate than those in the fiction of Shirley Jackson or Ramsey Campbell. He has not as yet embraced the zombie. In contrast, McGrath's fiction tests the boundaries of what we recognize as 'Gothic' and, far from abandoning 'the conventional props of the Gothic', he tends to use them in creative and parodic ways, as did fellow contributor to *The New Gothic* Angela Carter. Her story 'The Lady of the House of Love' (in a 1979 collection of rewritten folk tales, *The Bloody Chamber*), for example, presents a poignant portrait of a female vampire which exposes the tawdry artificiality of those very props.

Until recently, parody (like Gothic) has been considered a debased mode of writing. It is only since the early 1990s that work by critics such as Linda Hutcheon, Margaret Rose and Simon Dentith has claimed some sophistication for parodic writing, arguing that, in foregrounding its own textuality, parody represents part of a complex cultural dialogue.[18] In the later fiction, ghosts of 'the props of the genre' manifest themselves in different and more subtle representations of decay and transgression. In McGrath's work, an inclination towards Gothic excess remains in tension with a sceptical and ironic sensibility.

McGrath is well read in Gothic literature. He has acknowledged the influence of a host of writers, most notably Herman Melville, F. Scott Fitzgerald, Robert Louis Stevenson, Emily Brontë, Joseph Conrad and Bram Stoker as well as Edgar Allan Poe.[19] He is familiar with a tradition that has explored ways of giving shape to the forbidden, the unspeakable, the secret and the haunted. In its representation of transgression and decay the Gothic shows disorder and dismemberment, both physical and mental. It is balanced precariously between tragedy and comedy; its embrace of excess means that many Gothic tales are, in the words of Chris Baldick, 'already halfway to sending themselves up'.[20] McGrath's narrative technique in the earlier novels carries many of the markers of the postmodern; the double coding inherent in parody is, as Linda Hutcheon has pointed out, linked to the ironic stance of postmodernism.[21] A number of critics have pointed out the postmodern impulse in Gothic writing. Andrew Smith suggests that 'postmodernism seems to be peculiarly suited to the Gothic because it questions the notion that one inhabits a coherent or otherwise abstractly rational world'.[22] For Allan Lloyd Smith, 'what underlyingly links the Gothic with the postmodern is an aesthetic of anxiety and perplexity, as similar responses to the confusing new order – or should that be the new *dis*order?'[23] The dialectic between order and disorder and the power dynamics of the struggle between them characterize all McGrath's fiction, from the earliest darkly comic parodies in the short stories and the novel *The Grotesque* through to the story of his psychiatrist narrator Charlie Weir's inner conflict in the 2008 novel, *Trauma*.

Writing about the work of a living author presents several challenges. Although criticism since Barthes can never again use biographical information naively to validate readings of texts, the status of such information needs to be considered. McGrath is extraordinarily generous with his time and has been willing to give numerous interviews over the years, in which the same questions have been posed to him in various forms about the impulses behind his work. He is also reflective about the creative process and willing to comment on material that he has consciously employed.[24] In the following pages due weight has been given to his views as they have been expressed in various contexts. His engagement with the Gothic tradition, one informed by current critical debates, is distinctive and conscious. What he has to say, however, has been set alongside other readings of his work. A contextualization of the fiction in relation to literary traditions, the contemporary cultural and social context and McGrath's own sense of a writing identity all inform this book. Critical approaches from Gothic studies that seem to be appropriate and helpful in particular instances have been adopted, rather than a tightly focused theoretical lens.[25]

Certain key critical concepts have emerged from the recent evolution of Gothic studies. Two terms that appear repeatedly in the studies of the last twenty years are 'the uncanny' and 'the abject'; both concepts provide interesting perspectives on McGrath's fiction. Psychoanalytic critics have turned to Freud's influential essay, 'The Uncanny', in order to theorize the unsettling affect generated by the Gothic. Although Freud's terms '*heimlich*' and '*unheimlich*' do not translate comfortably into English, their pairing emphasizes the interrelatedness of the familiar and the unfamiliar, the circular effect whereby what is found to be strange and alienating is also recognized as already known. Thus, the boundary between the homely (*heimlich*) and the unhomely or uncanny (*unheimlich*) is radically unstable. As Nicholas Royle suggests: 'The uncanny has to do with a strangeness of framing and borders, an experience of liminality.'[26] Thus, the 'transgression' that so preoccupies McGrath is imbued with the uncanny. Even those critics who identify the limitations of psychoanalytic approaches to the Gothic find this term useful in discussing the ways in which Gothic gives shape to that which may not be directly spoken in a culture. Historical studies have helped to illuminate the cultural and historical inflection of the uncanny.[27]

The same is true of Kristeva's concept of the abject, a concept also concerned with boundaries, which many scholars have found invaluable in discussing the effects of horror. Although McGrath may not easily be categorized as a horror writer, his identification of 'decay' as a key element in the Gothic means that its presence may be felt in his fiction, sometimes in surprising contexts. Kristeva's 1982 book *Powers of Horror: An Essay on Abjection* has been seen to have particular relevance to Gothic writing by a number of critics. Horror and revulsion, she argues, are an echo of our early anxieties, surrounding the separation from the mother, that involve insecurity about materiality and the borders of the self. Abjection within the Gothic text frequently signifies both fear concerning the breakdown of culturally constructed boundaries of identity at a particular historical moment, and an attempt to shore them up. Oral abjection, one of the three broad categories of the abject (along with waste and sexual difference), is perhaps the most clearly marked by cultural difference through social taboo. What is considered edible in one culture may not be thought fit for eating in another; the almost (but not quite) universal taboo on cannibalism is made thematic in some of McGrath's early fiction and remains as a haunting presence (as it does in so many Gothic texts) through traces of vampirism. As Nicholas Royle reminds us, for Freud cannibalism is 'the taboo desire *par excellence*' and 'psychoanalysis gets started, in so far as it can and must get started, only on the base of a theory of cannibalism'.[28]

The abject writ large in social terms, Kristeva suggests, is that which:

disturbs identity, system, order. What does not respect borders, positions, rules. The in-between, the ambiguous, the composite. The traitor, the liar, the criminal with a good conscience, the shameless rapist, the killer who claims he is a saviour ... Any crime, because it draws attention to the fragility of the law, is abject, but premeditated crime, cunning murder, hypocritical revenge are even more so because they heighten the display of such fragility.[29]

Jerrold E. Hogle and Robert Miles have shown how Kristevan theory may be used to explore the way in which representations of the abject in some Gothic texts relate to discourses and cultural values at a particular historical moment.[30] This approach, as Hogle points out, allows us to 'connect psychological repression with the cultural ways of constructing coherent senses of "self" that initially made and still make the very concept of repression conceivable'.[31] Kristeva's concept of the abject thereby becomes a way of defining how shared constructions of 'otherness' derive from shared cultural values: you may know a culture by what it 'throws off'.

In exploring what is abjected in drawing the boundaries of dominant cultures, Gothic criticism of the last twenty-five years has often been concerned with three elements identified by David Punter as lying at the heart of Gothic writing: the concept of paranoia, the notion of the barbaric and the nature of the taboo – 'aspects of the terrifying to which Gothic constantly, and hauntedly, returns'.[32] The ongoing debate in Gothic studies about psychoanalysis and historicity (and whether or not they are mutually exclusive) provides a framework for the discussion of McGrath's fiction, which characteristically pre-empts a psychoanalytic reading. It does this by questioning – both implicitly and explicitly – the validity of psychoanalysis as a mastering discourse while offering a postmodern critique of history and histories. Indeed, McGrath is a particularly interesting writer to consider in the light of this debate in Gothic criticism, which became crystallized following the intervention of Chris Baldick and Robert Mighall in 2000. Their argument is summed up in their opening salvo: 'In our view, Gothic Criticism has abandoned any credible historical grasp upon its object, which it has tended to reinvent in the image of its own projected intellectual goals of psychological "depth" and political "subversion".'[33] They are particularly critical of the depth model of psychoanalytic criticism that analyses the text in order to uncover deep-seated – and usually bourgeois – anxieties. Anne Williams has noted how many Freudian readings of Gothic tend to be reductive, and unsophisticated, resembling 'a kind of

Freudian Easter Egg Hunt' for lurking complexes and delusions.[34] For William Patrick Day, Gothicism and Freudianism are different but related responses to 'the problems of selfhood and identity, sexuality and pleasure, fear and anxiety as they manifest themselves in the nineteenth and early twentieth centuries'. 'The Gothic', he suggests, 'arises out of the immediate needs of the reading public to escape from conventional life and articulate and define the turbulence of their psychic existence. We may see Freud as the intellectual counterpart of this process.'[35] Psychoanalysis itself has been acknowledged by a number of critics as a Gothic discourse. Alexandra Warwick's essay in the recent *Routledge Companion to Gothic*, for example, suggests that, just as 'Freud's theories of the structure and processes of the psyche have been used more than any other to read the Gothic . . . it is equally plausible to reverse the terms of the analogy, and to use the Gothic to read his work.' 'If Gothic', she continues, 'can be thought of as interrogating the anxiety of the influence of the past on the present, then Freud's work can also be defined in these terms, persistently concerned with the question of what is dead, what survives and how things are revived.'[36]

Not only is McGrath well read in Gothic fiction, he is also well informed about Freudian psychology (an interest originating in his background as the son of an eminent psychiatrist).[37] In two of his novels (*Asylum* and *Trauma*) McGrath makes psychiatry (the medical cousin of psychoanalysis) thematic, pointing to its ambiguous status as a mastering discourse. Indeed, medicine itself is represented Gothically in McGrath's fiction; the doctor in McGrath is a Gothic figure, from physically monstrous Cadwallader in 'Blood and Water' to the deeply flawed Dr Haggard. It is, however, a historicized medicine, in which the assumed omniscience of the medical man is undermined by the limits of his historical location. Indeed, all of McGrath's novels, even those overtly playing with the monstrous and parodic, are firmly rooted in time and place. The past weighs heavily on his characters, returning often to haunt them, and on his narratives, challenging his contemporary readers to reflect on its legacy.

Madness – a recurrent theme in the fiction and explicitly addressed in *Spider* and *Asylum* – is always specifically located and contextualized. Moreover, mental disorder is rendered in McGrath's fiction through ordered and elegant prose, so that reading about such extremes of human experience becomes a matter of aesthetics. His skill in tackling the technical challenges of representing madness is related to his capacity to negotiate the finely balanced boundaries between inter-textuality, irony and pastiche. Often, when the reader assumes that the techniques of realism are being utilized, the ground is at its most treacherous; in some respects, *Asylum* is more Gothic than *The Grotesque*. His first-person narrators inevitably give their own per-spectives: through the voices of Dennis Cleg in *Spider* and Edward Haggard in *Dr Haggard's Disease*, the reader is seduced into seeing the world through the eyes of the mentally disturbed. Sometimes in the telling of others' stories these narrators by implication tell their own (Gin Rathbone in *Port Mungo* and Peter Cleave in *Asylum*, for example). McGrath sometimes adopts the cool scientific tones of the medical practitioner in order to expose the shakiness of the foundations of such purportedly objective discourse. Through the voices of Peter Cleave, of the anonymous narrator of 'Ground Zero' (the last story in *Ghost Town*) and, most recently, of Charlie Weir in *Trauma*, psychiatry is shown to be more deeply involved with its subjects than it would claim – or than the reader finds comfortable.

McGrath's fiction is charted chronologically in this book for two reasons. For those interested in a particular text, this will provide focused discussion; more importantly, perhaps, this approach demon-strates the ways in which themes and tropes in the earlier fiction have found more complex and subtle expression in the later work, as the exploration of the haunting effects of history (both personal and public) takes a transatlantic turn. Chapter 1 explores the early short stories, identifying tropes and themes that signal a parodic engagement with other Gothic writing, some of which surface again in the later fiction. Clearly, homage is being paid to various ante-cedents in these tales where the past and future are more in evidence than the present. Edgar Allan Poe haunts the pages of many: in the decadent or decayed mansions of 'Marmilion' and 'Blood and Water' and the live entombment of the narrator of 'The Smell', for example. The colonial Gothic of writers like Somerset Maugham and H. Rider Haggard is echoed in stories like 'The Lost Explorer' and 'The Black Hand of the Raj' and 'Blood Disease'. The transgression of boundaries characteristic of all Gothic fiction manifests itself either horrifically or comically (and sometimes both) in all the stories. Crime takes a funny turn in 'The Arnold Crombeck Story', and perverse bodies of unstable identity are in evidence in 'The Angel', 'Blood and Water' and 'The Skewer'; cannibalism makes an appearance in 'The Boot's Tale' and, more obliquely, 'Blood Disease'. Some of the more eccentric features of earlier Gothic fiction and film are in evidence: monkeys (in the tradition of Sheridan LeFanu's short story 'Green Tea') make a sinister and enigmatic appearance, both in 'Blood Disease' and in 'Marmilion'; hands – either disembodied (as in 'Hand of a Wanker' or attached to the wrong part of the anatomy (as in 'The Black Hand of the Raj') – take on their own agency. Apocalyptic themes are approached through body horror and black comedy in 'The Boot's Tale' and 'The E(rot)ic Potato'. In these early tales, too, figures that will recur in the later fiction make their first appearance: the orthodox medical man (in the peripheral figure of the surgeon, Mr Piker-Smith,[38] in 'The Lost Explorer' and the gross and ill-fated figure of Dr Cadwallader in 'Blood and Water') and the psychoanalyst, in various manifestations, in 'The Skewer'. The tortured artist who becomes a central figure in *Asylum* and *Port Mungo* is the focus in 'Lush Triumphant'. This is a story set in New York, a location even more decadently realized in 'The Angel' and one to which McGrath was to return in his later fiction. The latter story exemplifies the vexed relationship Gothic has always had with religion and which also surfaces in different ways in 'Ambrose Syme', with its murderous paedophilic priest, and 'Hand of a Wanker', a tale of Babylon on the Hudson. The preoccupation with perverse and unstable bodies that will surface again in the later fiction provides the thematic focus for 'The Angel' and 'Blood and Water'. McGrath's first novel, *The Grotesque* (1989), is also discussed in chapter 1, with particular reference to its self-conscious pastiche of the Gothic.

Chapter 2 considers the three novels of the 1990s, *Spider* (1990), *Dr Haggard's Disease* (1993) and *Asylum* (1996), which explore madness from different perspectives. McGrath has explained:

> In my first stories I sort of stumbled into the first-person narrator which turned into the unreliable narrator. What I'd actually done was reinvent the wheel, but at the time I didn't know that and it felt like an exciting breakthrough. After that it was a short step to creating narrators whose unreliability is a psychological dysfunction.[39]

These novels are less playful than the stories and darkly haunted by Gothic in their representation of taboo and transgression. All are set in a murky and eccentric mid twentieth-century England. This retro-spective emphasis provides a setting through which McGrath, himself a child of the 1950s, draws on his own background to provide the stuff of fiction. A childhood spent on the estate of Broadmoor, one of Britain's high-security mental hospitals, and a father happy to share anecdotes from his work as its chief psychiatrist at the dinner table meant that he had plenty of material.[40] The third of these novels is, as its title suggests, set in such a hospital. It is in this novel that the figure of the artist appears again, this time as a patient and convicted killer.

McGrath was to devote an entire novel to the artist in *Port Mungo* (2004), which is one of the novels discussed in chapter 3. This chapter considers the first three works from the twenty-first century, *Martha Peake* (2000) and *Ghost Town* (2005) as well as *Port Mungo*. In this period of his fiction, issues of historicity, national and personal identity and the figure of the artist become central concerns. *Martha Peake* takes a final self-reflexive look at earlier period Gothic as a way of enacting the abandonment of a culturally haunted England in favour of the New World, a movement that parallels McGrath's own departure for North America after university. As the later fiction shows, however, haunting is not confined to the Old World. The weight of history and how it has been constructed continue to make themselves felt in the present of this fiction. These novels and stories continue to probe the haunting of the past and, in so doing, are themselves haunted by ghosts of the Gothic. In the Afterword, McGrath's repudiation of the term 'Gothic' is considered in relation to his most recent novel, *Trauma*, together with the implications for his future work.

1

Playing with Gothic

ഃ)ൠ

The Short Stories

The motifs, themes and modes of writing to be found in McGrath's later fiction have their genesis in the early short stories. The precarious and sometimes gleeful balancing of comedy and horror in many of them implies a consciousness of the hybridity of Gothic, used to advantage in a distinctive way. In an interview with Gilles Menegaldo in 1997, McGrath acknowledged his parodic relationship with Gothic conventions in the early work:

> the Gothic genre is a mature genre; it's a mannered genre, and to work in it with any real freshness or originality is difficult. My first impulse was to play with its very well established conventions; that inevitably became a form of pastiche as I exaggerated motifs, images that had already been well exaggerated by two centuries of development.[1]

McGrath's earliest fiction takes the form of the short story. Most of the early work appears in the collection *Blood and Water and Other Tales*, published in 1988. Two later stories were published in 1991, one in an anthology entitled *I Shudder at Your Touch*, edited by Michelle Slung, and the other in Morrow and McGrath's anthology, *The New Gothic*. The latter story, 'The Smell', is distinctive for the absence of specific setting, taking place entirely within an unidentified house and involving nameless characters. In contrast, most of the short fiction is clearly sited in time and place. McGrath's own transatlantic identity is represented in his choices of setting and the different inflection of the English and American contexts. His later fiction draws on the same dual identity: the first four novels are set in mid twentieth-century England; the 2000 novel, *Martha Peake*, makes the representation of the relationship between England and the United States thematic, and the subsequent fiction is largely set in America. In the short stories and the novels, the two countries both appear as freighted with a textual history. McGrath's use of parody in the early fiction, his exaggeration of 'motifs, images that had already been well exaggerated by two centuries of development', signals, it may be argued, an engagement with the wider implications of Gothic in its different contexts. Individual tales of transgression and decay may point to larger stories of cultural abjection and crisis. Thus, the Gothic themes of these short stories – vampirism; unstable bodies; fears of degeneration; violation of taboo – resonate beyond the boundaries of the fiction. Often they are inflected through McGrath's own distinctive preoccupations: the problematic nature of medical practice (specifically psychiatry), madness and what it means to be an artist.

The influence of Edgar Allan Poe, whom McGrath sees as a key figure in the development of Gothic fiction, is clearly at work in many of the short stories. Asked to guest-edit an issue on the new Gothic in 1990 for the recently founded literary magazine *Conjunctions*, McGrath wrote in his afterword:

> It is with Poe that we first see the Gothic shifting away from an emphasis on props and sets – dark forests and lugubrious caverns, skeletons and thunderstorms – and towards a particular sensibility characterized by transgressive tendencies and extreme distortions of perception and affect. Poe's genius lies in his recognition of the sorts of structural analogies possible between the trappings and the sensibility, than in the deftness with which he splices them together.[2]

The introduction to *The New Gothic* pays tribute to Poe for turning the Gothic inward 'to explore extreme states of psychological disturb- ance' (p. xi). McGrath's contribution to this 1991 collection, 'The

Smell', lacks the comic dimension of many of his early stories and is now described by him in retrospect as 'a very nasty, very dirty piece of work, almost fecal'.[3] 'The abject', as defined by Kristeva, is often to be found in his fiction as a mode of representing madness.[4] This Poe-esque tale is told by one of McGrath's characteristic first-person narrators. In it, a petty domestic tyrant with a passion for order and a penchant for abuse becomes increasingly paranoid as he detects a smell that is evident only to him. The other members of his household are oblivious to this smell, but not unconnected with it. Running 'a stern regime' and predisposed to punish any infraction (in a manner he does not specify), he begins to sense it after crossing a threshold in oppressive behaviour.[5] He wakes his sleeping children to punish them in some dreadful way that is left to the reader's imagination, 'watching the horror from somewhere outside one's own body' (246). He is then compelled to pursue the smell ('I was drawn to the smell like a moth to a flame, it was *pulling me in*' (246)) to the chimney, where he has already detected 'a sweet and viscous liquid dripping into the fireplace' (244). Trying to reach it by climbing up the chimney, he becomes irretrievably wedged, in a version of the live burial that Eve Kosofsky Sedgwick in her study of Gothic conventions has identified as one of the preoccupations of Gothic narratives – a trope used by Poe, for example, in 'The Cask of Amontillado'.[6]

Images of secrets buried or holed up in some way recur in the early stories, and the chimney was to be used later by McGrath in *Spider*, when his narrator hides his notebooks in the chimney in his attic bedroom. The physical details of putrefaction in 'The Smell' recall the oleaginous quality of what Kelly Hurley, after William Hope Hodgson, calls the 'abhuman' in late Victorian Gothic fiction, the entropic body.[7] What is new here is the self-destructive nature of the experience and the way in which an obsessive desire for order leads to the ultimate entropy of death. The family romance is translated into the death wish in horrifying fashion, with the abuse inflicted on the disempowered of the household turned back on the abuser. The 'milky feeling' he describes in relation to punishing the children becomes transmuted into the final simile of the story in this narrative from beyond the grave (or, in his case, chimney), as he suffocates, 'stuffed up my chimney like a dirty cork in a bottle of rancid milk'

(247). The image of milk points to childhood and suggests some shameful secret which is never divulged.

Jerrold E. Hogle offers a reading of this story informed by his argument that the Gothic reflects the fragmentation of signs and artefacts theorized by Baudrillard as characteristic of postmodernity:

> Here is strong evidence joining with Baudrillard's that a culture of pure simulation, especially when it is imported into the heart of the home as a system of management, is indeed a culture of death in its very efforts to transcend the death of the body and of the self.[8]

In Hogle's psychoanalytic reading, the pull towards the chimney in 'The Smell' is representative of 'an unconscious longing for the body and the mother (even in a death wish)', and the story challenges the reader 'to consider which is more Gothically monstrous: the re-insistence of the body with its primordial and final liquidity or the distancing and denial of that Real in systematic simulations that once made the Gothic possible as a form of fiction and drama?'[9] What Hogle's highly theorized reading does not consider is another aspect of the uncanny at work in the story: it may be read as one of retributive justice, in which the disciplining and punishing rituals are themselves transgressive and in their turn are punished through supernatural intervention.

The uncanny is ever-present in varying forms in McGrath's fictions. His English settings present a recognizable England, usually in the middle decades of the twentieth century, but one that is always sinister and imbued with the uncanny. In the short stories, the narrative voices play competing discourses against each other. The homeliness of this England is disturbed by the strange or exotic in various forms; in Freudian terms, the *unheimlich* irrupts into the *heimlich*. Scientific discourse, and often specifically medical discourse, is juxtaposed with the bizarre or superstitious, often to darkly comic effect. These stories lay the groundwork for the territory of McGrath's first four novels, all of which are set in this period, a time in many ways remote from the world of today but within living memory. These settings are not, however, those of the realist novel; they are more akin to a past that is accessed through its fiction. The stories invoke a chronotope, to use Bakhtin's term,[10] that is already highly textualized, but do so with critical difference; there is, in other words, a postmodern parodic quality to them, 'repetition with critical difference', in Linda Hutcheon's formulation.

In *Blood and Water*, the golden age of British crime fiction is recognized in 'The Arnold Crombeck Story', which tells a tale of transgression through criminal ingenuity. Although set in 1954, a decade or two later than the heyday of the genre, it is reminiscent of the work of writers like Margery Allingham, Dorothy L. Sayers and Agatha Christie, and provides both a twist at the end and a conservative recuperation of legality, when Crombeck does not succeed in his final fiendish attempt at murder and meets his due punishment. Its villain, however, is also an example of the mentally disturbed murderer who will appear again in S*pider* and *Asylum*. Known as the 'death gardener', he describes his ideal garden in lyric terms.[11] Gardening assumes an important role in the novels *Spider* and *Asylum*; within the asylum, in both of them, gardens are associated with equilibrium. But they are an ambiguous symbol in McGrath's fiction. They can also be associated with derangement and death. Crombeck may describe with bright eyes his 'God-given' garden, an English country garden, and yet have murder in his heart and in his hands (77).

'God' often signifies delusion in McGrath's fiction. In 'Ambrose Syme' he draws upon his own unhappy experience of Stoneyhurst, the austere Catholic school where he had spent some time as a boy. He is also acknowledging a number of literary precursors. Colin Green has noted the influence of Mervyn Peake on this story, in which the school is called 'Ravengloom' and the Catholic Church is an everthreatening and sinister presence.[12] The raven in the name reminds us that Poe, too, is never far away in this early fiction. The setting maps on to Stoneyhurst's location in the north-west of England, but the description of the topography also evokes the Dickensian world of *Hard Times*, with the Preston-inspired Coketown renamed 'Gryme'. The Gothic edifice of Ravengloom reminds us of the historical origins of Gothic fiction, what Victor Sage has called 'Horror Fiction in the Protestant Tradition'.[13] Its transgressive priest, Syme, is – as his Christian name suggests – a latter-day Ambrosio, his crimes as shocking as those of Lewis's monk. Yet he is treated more sympathetically than his eighteenth-century precursor, by a narrator who recognizes the foundations of repression that have made him a paedophile and murderer; he is shown to be himself a victim. Twenty years and more since the publication of this story, so many accounts of abuse in its institutions have emerged that the Catholic Church finds itself in crisis. The history in this instance seems to be as Gothic as the fiction. This story's powerful representation of the link between repression and transgression reveals a cultural haunting at work; other stories explore further dimensions of the cultural haunting of England.

In the figure of Father Mungo, elderly rector of Ravengloom, McGrath's preoccupation with the colonial aspect of British history is apparent. The name of this benevolent figure ('who was still remembered with awe and affection by the natives of the Zambesi Basin' (68)) is derived from that of the great explorer Mungo Park. McGrath has suggested that the African motif in his early fiction was 'probably an outgrowth of [his] interest in pasticing nineteenth-century fictions', and that in his writing 'Africa became a symbol of the unconscious, the unpredictable, the chaotic'.[14] The influence of Conrad is clear and, indeed, McGrath has identified *Heart of Darkness* as one of the books that has given him greatest pleasure.[15] The figure of the explorer appears again in 'The Lost Explorer'. The cultural history of colonial exploration here finds expression in the heart of the bourgeois family, where it represents an exotic 'otherness' in the imagination of a girl on the threshold of puberty. Like many Gothic tales, this story works within a liminal space. Evelyn Piker-Smith's encounter with the exotic operates in the territory where realism gives way to fantasy, and the boundary between the two is unstable.[16] This is signalled in the opening sentence, as 'one fresh and gusty day in the damp autumn of her twelfth year Evelyn found a lost explorer in the garden of her parents' London home' (17). In another inflection of the garden trope, the explorer's tent is pitched in the wild area at the bottom of the garden, an area that is described in terms of a Gothic desolation reminiscent of the sexually charged dream of Manderley in the opening of Daphne du Maurier's Gothic novel *Rebecca*: 'The rest of the garden beyond the pond was a tangled and overgrown mass of rhododendron bushes, into whose labyrinthine depths, since the death of the old gardener, only Evelyn now ventured' (20). The trivialities of life carry on in their humdrum way in the Piker-Smiths' bourgeois home, providing a contrast with the suffering of the explorer in his tropical delirium.

The two realities exist side by side for Evelyn, however, and both are narrated as such; only in the liminal area is there an acknowledgement of Evelyn's imagination, as she thinks of the three white sheets billowing in the wind on the washing-line as sails on 'a great ship shouldering on to the tropics' (21). The narrative juxtaposes this with the next sentence, as she picks up 'a jar containing a pickled thumb that Daddy had given her' (21). Given the sexual connotations of hands in these early stories (in 'Hand of a Wanker', for example), it is difficult to read this other than in terms of a rather crude phallic symbol. It is, of course, not surprising in this house (Evelyn's father is one of McGrath's many medical men), where the topics of conversation at the dinner table include 'a rather interesting colostomy [her father had] performed', after which 'Uncle Frank made some quips which might, in a non medical household, have been taken in rather bad taste' (24). The body in this context is a masculinized domain.

In spite of his supernatural status, the explorer has for Evelyn a fully realized materiality in the text; there is nothing overtly spectral about him. From his 'creased map of the upper reaches of the Congo' to his torn mosquito net, he is accompanied by the trappings of his calling (17). In the liminal zone between childhood and adulthood, Evelyn shares with the explorer an alternative reality, aligning herself with neither female sexuality (as personified by Aunt Vera), domesticity (in the shape of her 'plump, tweedy' mother) nor the male doctors, who represent a banal rationality. Through her fantasy, the reader is offered an alternative perspective on an aspect of British history. Listening to Uncle Frank's rambling account of Stanley's adventures in the Congo, Evelyn glimpses over his shoulder the explorer, his 'unshaven face deeply etched with gullies of suffering' and his clothes looking 'extraordinarily ragged and filthy against the beige flowered wallpaper of the hallway' (25). When the explorer dies shortly afterwards, Evelyn stashes his body in the corner of a closet and tries to get rid of 'the stink of a man too long in the jungle'. In one of the many comic turns in these early stories, her mother attributes the 'funny smell' the next morning to Evelyn's 'hockey things', thus creating a bathetic closure to the explorer's sojourn in the

Piker-Smiths' residence (28). After burying him with his possessions in the garden, Evelyn sees him occasionally as a spectral presence under a full moon, but by the time she has decided to become a doctor (at the age of fourteen and a half), 'he disappeared from her life completely' (31).

If this is a fantasy, it is (with its details of anthropophagous pygmies and a 'creased and sweat-stained' map (30–1)) a male adventure fantasy. Evelyn's decision to become a doctor – entering into the male territory signified by the thumb – coincides with the disappearance of the explorer as she finds an adult role to pursue. The immediacy of her experience and her compassion towards the suffering man, as she tends to his needs, suggest, however, other possibilities for the medical profession than the smug indifference exemplified by the male doctors in the story. Hovering over both the fantasy and the quotidian reality, however, is a deeper fear, that of regression and entropy. In the wild zone of the garden, the wood-shed harbours 'three substances, sacking, wood and the earth beneath the rotten wood, [which] had begun to coalesce, as if in attempting, in their nostalgia for some primeval state of slime, to abandon structure and identity, all that could distinguish or separate them' (29). In the face of such forces the ephemeral nature of human lives is thrown into sharp relief, as are the ways in which they are recorded. The insubstantiality of textuality is represented by faded photographs in the shed, in which

> barely a trace could now be detected of the humans who had stood, once, before the camera, vital, one presumes, and alive. It was as though they had died in the bad air, the malaria, of that neglected little corner of the garden, the thin dusty air of the old shed, within which everything must devolve to a fused state of formless unity . . . (30)

A less ambiguously comic treatment of the Englishwoman and Britain's colonial past is to be found in 'The Black Hand of the Raj', which adopts an earlier setting, that of Victorian India. In this story the motif of the hand is central; its synecdochic quality places it in a tradition of hands with sinister import in Gothic texts.[17] This hand acts autonomously and with lascivious intent, as does its American counterpart in 'Hand of a Wanker', but in this instance it is also murderous. Parodying the tradition of earlier stories of the Raj, from

Kipling to Forster, and set in 1897, the story relates the experience of its young Victorian heroine, Lucy Hepplewhite. The narrator speaks from a mid twentieth-century perspective and the story opens with an academic Marxist discourse on the economic foundations of imperialism; this is soon explicitly set aside in favour of an exploration of the 'soft face of imperialism', which had enabled Europeans to discover passion in torrid climates. The narrator then sets the reader up for a tale in which 'darker forces' are at work and 'the encounter of East and West, of the sensual and rational' has a less satisfactory resolution (32). At this point the narrator displays the stylistic versatility of the parodist by adopting the language of romantic excess; Lucy becomes a 'flower of Victorian maidenhood', whose 'dark eyes are misted and shining' and whose 'small pearly teeth gleam like stars' from between 'her soft lips' (33).

Lucy is also represented as belonging to the tradition of intrepid colonial Englishwomen: she is 'a girl of pretty stout kidney' (34). Even for such a heroine, however, what follows is horrific. The erotic awakening implied by her expectations of her imminent marriage takes a most peculiar turn, when the reason for her fiancé Cecil's reluctance to remove his pith helmet is revealed. Underneath it, a hand is growing out of his head. This is the result of the laying-on of hands by a mysterious little old man 'with a bald head and a loin-cloth', a figure that bizarrely evokes the image of Gandhi (36). Cecil has medication to keep the hand sedated; tragically, this seems in-effective on the night of Lucy's arrival, so that she finds him dead in the morning, strangled by his uncanny appendage. She has dreamed about the hand, which had taken on an erotic agency: 'it writhed and twisted and beckoned and pointed, it throbbed and undulated like a serpent, and performed gestures of an unspeakably lewd nature' (38). What follows is an act that is comically abject: the hand consum-mates the relationship as Lucy 'moan[s] in the shadows of the body of her lover'. When she recovers, she observes that 'Cecil was beginning to go bad' (40); the Victorians' fear of female sexuality and their obsession with death are thus linked. The doctor's diagnosis is 'Black Hand of the Raj', 'some sort of wog curse' that is always fatal (40).

At Cecil's funeral the blackly comic effect is sustained by the obser-vation, 'she counted no fewer than seven Englishmen conspicuous for not having removed their headgear'. Lucy returns to England

and becomes a nun, praying for her dead fiancé and 'wondering, in her heart of hearts, what, exactly, was the nature of the sin she had committed' (42). For the narrator, this is history, hence the quasi-objectivity of the story's frame; Lucy had died twenty-five years earlier, having lived out the remaining half-century of her life within the convent, oblivious of the upheavals of history.[18] Through its comic take on the violation of Victorian propriety and the Gothic auton-omy of the wayward hand, 'The Black Hand of the Raj' constitutes a playful engagement with fears both of the exotic and of female sexuality and serves to suggest the inherent instability of imperialism.

'Blood Disease' evokes the spectres of Empire through some of the other conventions of popular Gothic fiction, particularly that of the vampire, to create a story that confounds the reader's expectations. The vampiric trope appears in various guises in McGrath's later work. In contrast with developments in vampire fiction over the last thirty-five years that have made vampirism seem almost like an alternative lifestyle choice (by endowing the vampire with its own subjectivity and emphasizing its glamorous qualities),[19] McGrath's vampiric presences signify a negative and destructive otherness. In the later fiction, they tend to emanate from the minds of his characters or exist as traces written on human bodies, as in *Port Mungo* and *Ghost Town* (see chapter 3). 'Blood Disease' is both a vampire story and an anti-vampire story. Its narrative lays trails of false clues in a process of wrong-footing its reader, and refuting their expectations. It also demonstrates one of McGrath's characteristic techniques, that of juxtaposing different discourses in order to highlight the short-comings of each. Set in the mid 1930s, in the rural south of England, it reveals the practices of rustic English folk to be more bizarre and more violent than those of the pygmies of the equatorial rainforest, whom the returning anthropologist William Clack-Herman (other-wise known as 'Congo Bill') has left behind.

The dominant motif of blood in this story is represented through both scientific and Gothic discourses. While cautioning the reader with the opening line, 'This is probably how it happened', the opening paragraph accounts in scientific terms for the debilitated malarial state in which Congo Bill arrives at Southampton (84). What follows is a detailed account of what happens when someone is bitten by a malaria-carrying mosquito. When a flea from the colobus monkey that Bill had brought back as a gift for his son Frank bites the boy, the reader is led to assume, therefore, that this is significant. Set against the scientific discourse is a set of markers that parody the vampire tale. The Clack-Hermans (Frank, Bill and his wife Virginia) stop for the night at an old inn called 'The Blue Bat'. As its name suggests, this rustic hostelry, in spite of its reputation for 'good beds, fine kitchen and ... extensive cellar' (86), is not to be regarded as a place of safety. Another guest arrives, a Ronald Dexter with whom Virginia has had an earlier relationship. His manservant, Clutch, is a grotesque figure who gives the impression of 'a monstrous fetus' (86) and who seems to fear the dangerous possibilities of the English countryside. Seeing him slip a crucifix into his master's evening clothes, Ronald asks him if he imagines he will be set upon by vampires, to which his manservant replies, 'One cannot be too careful ... we are not in London, sir' (87). Other false clues suggesting vampirism are given; at one point it seems possible that Ronald might be the victim of Virginia, who bears some of the markers of the vampire herself: 'Her dress was of dead-white satin and cut extremely low. She was wearing a rope of pearls; her face was as white as her pearls, and her lips a vivid scarlet' (90). Instead, as he leaves her bedroom, he is set upon by two men from the public bar, 'flabby men with waxy skin and big, soft faces as round and pale as the rising moon' (94). Virginia awakes to find herself, like Stoker's Jonathan Harker, 'surrounded by large pale women whose eyes glittered at her with an unnatural brilliance' (101).

When the secret of 'The Blue Bat' is revealed to the reader, a secret that causes Ronald, Virginia and Frank to be dispatched and ex-sanguinated in the cellar (events described in gruesome detail), scientific discourse then comes into the ascendancy again. The Gothic figure of Clutch has already realized that the strange appearance of the people in the public bar can be explained by the diagnosis of pernicious anaemia and has 'hiked off toward Reading, where somebody at the Royal Berkshire Hospital, he felt sure, would take his story seriously' (102). The appropriately named Dr Gland ('who'd once read a paper on iatrophobia and sanguinivorous dementia [bloodlust] in per-nicious anaemia' (102)) confirms what the reader has already been told, that events at the inn are subject to rational explanation. As with malaria, there is a disintegration of the red blood-cells; unlike malaria, the condition produces a group identity, hence the 'cell of untreated anaemics' (98) at 'The Blue Bat' preying on unsuspecting travellers and their corollary, the unsuspecting reader.

Such rationalization, however, is also treacherous because elements of the uncanny remain in the story. In characteristic Gothic mode, the boundary between life and death is rendered unstable. The narrative is interspersed with Congo Bill's malarial delusions, in which he is back in the paradise of the Congo forest. The narrative also describes how, in effect, he had been brought back from the dead by the pygmies, who have three categories of death: as well as 'dead', there is 'dead forever' and 'absolutely dead' (101). A similar resurrection takes place with the monkey, who appears to die in the course of the story. Frank has been befriended by the landlord's daughter, Meg, who had initially terrified him with her approach, although the 'slow, heavy clump-clump-clump' is revealed to be created by an orthopaedic boot (93). It is Meg who dresses the monkey in a 'tiny gown of white lace' and helps him place it in a shoebox for burial – in the cellar where the murders are taking place. The monkey's revival down in the cellar (it was 'clearly not dead forever' (103)) leads to Frank's discovery and his murder alongside his mother. The story ends with Congo Bill coming out of his delirium and spotting Meg making for the woods with the monkey on her shoulder. The figure of the monkey plays an uncanny role. Not the hallucinatory spectre of LeFanu's 'Green Tea', its status in this story is nonetheless liminal. It signifies the permeability of the boundary between life and death, as well as the frailty of human identity, in spite of the rational scientific discourse that has explained the bizarre events at the inn. In the 1930s England of this story, infection and degeneracy are endemic in the English countryside; the threat is not the exotic but the domestic. This is contained by medical science at the end of the story, but the uncanny figure of the monkey is unsettling, reminding the reader of the limitations in understanding of its rational practices.

While the murderous degeneracy of the 'cell of untreated anaemics' provides the horror of 'Blood Disease', madness in the English upper class is the satiric target of the parody of the later story 'Not Cricket', which also plays with the idea of the vampire.[20] The setting is a country house (Wallop Hall, 'a fine example of rustic Gothic' (119)[21]), where the butler is suggestively called Stoker. McGrath's propensity for selecting evocative names thus sets the frame for the fantasies of the story's narrator, Lady Hock, mistress of the Hall. She has taken herself off her medication, the nature of which is never specified but may be inferred from the hallucinations that then begin to beset her. This leads to her conviction that, in the person of Cleave, a cricketing visitor, she is entertaining not merely a demon bowler (who emasculates and sends off to hospital an inoffensive opponent with a fast ball to the testicles), but a vampire. In Lady Hock's eyes, Cleave possesses all the physical attributes of the Stokerian vampire: 'deep sunken eyes' in a 'disproportionately long face dominated by a huge, cadaverous jaw' are combined with 'a shock of jet-black hair, thickly oiled, that was brushed straight back from a sharp peak dead in the centre of a low cliff of overhanging forehead' (121–2). Moreover, she discerns 'a sort of red glow . . . deep in each of his eye sockets' (122) and his 'teeth shining with a nasty yellowish lustre' (124). Determined to protect her daughter, though also carried away by what Millie Williamson has identified as 'the lure of the vampire',[22] she determines to offer herself up to Cleave that night, but finds him sleeping. Admitting herself tempted, she instead hits him 'extremely hard with a piece of metal piping that the plumbers had left behind' and then hammers a meat skewer through his heart with that quintessential emblem of English country house recreation, a croquet mallet (130). It is only at the end of the story that she divulges that she is telling her story from the asylum where she is quite happy, playing bridge with her friend's daughter, who has been incarcerated for 'murdering the parish priest with a blunt axe in a moment of delusional psychosis' (120). The reader is left to speculate whether this has indeed been a vampire story or an everyday tale of an unfortunate outsider with a good bowling arm who happened, like Stoker's Dracula, to bear the markers of a different ethnicity.

In McGrath's fiction, the English upper classes tend to be both mad and murderous; the asylum, it would appear, is their natural home. It is the final destination of Sir Norman Percy in 'Blood and Water', the title story of the collection, whose crime has been to decapitate a visiting Harley Street doctor. In this story, some of the persistent concerns of McGrath's fiction may be discerned: the degeneracy of the upper classes; the limitations of the scientific perspective, specifically that of the medical profession; and a Gothic fascination with the instability of bodily forms. Sir Norman's ancestral home, 'Phlange', is, like 'Crook' in McGrath's first novel, *The Grotesque*, a place of grotesque perversity. Like many of the stories in the collection that bears its title, 'Blood and Water' demonstrates McGrath's skill in using the comic potential of the Gothic.[23] Domestic plumbing is used as an analogue for anatomy, as Sir Norman struggles with both an unreliable boiler and hermaphroditic developments in his wife's genitalia, a struggle that culminates in her suicide and his incarceration.[24] The punning link between plumbing and anatomy is sustained throughout (the estate handyman is called Tinkler), as the dispassionate narrative voice reconstructs the crime that lies at the centre of the story and invites the reader to view a series of scenes in phrases like 'now turn your eyes' and 'our first clear glimpse' (172, 173). The historical siting of the story is very precise: August 1936, 'a cloudless Friday afternoon' when 'England is at peace' (172), a point in history when 'the landed gentry is hardly prospering' (174).

The point of conflict in the story is Lady Percy's body. She is not, however, represented as abject but as an ethereal figure from romance, 'a pale woman in a white silk gown, utterly motionless and devoid of expression, gazing out over the copse of chestnuts on the brow of the distant hills, and into the deep sky beyond' (172) from her chamber, with its 'four-poster bed, spread with a fine-woven coverlet of medieval design' (181). In contrast, it is the doctor who is rendered as monstrous: grossly fat and androgynous in his own way, marked as monstrously feminine with 'wide, soft-nippled tyres of flesh', but (in keeping with the joking but sinister use of the plumbing metaphor) a 'little pink hose-end of a penis peeping out from below' (173). It is the doctor's proposal that Lady Percy's case should be written up in the *Lancet* as 'a scientific monograph' (177) and Sir Norman's fear that she will be subjected 'to the knife' (178) that precipitate the catastrophe. Suffering from the delusion that he is an Arthurian knight protecting his lady, the latter dispatches the foe with one plumber's tool ('a large spanner') and saws off his head with another. Thus, in comic parodic mode, using a crude phallic symbol, Sir Norman asserts his masculinity and mastery of his domain. The story's emphasis on the specular makes it particularly susceptible to a psychoanalytic reading. Freud's essay 'The Uncanny' identifies the fear of blinding as being symbolic of the fear of castration. Sir Norman, in presenting the doctor's bloody severed head to his lady, says: 'Show yourself to me' (181) and her 'deformity' is revealed. 'In deep psychotic territory' (182), Sir Norman does not realize until it is too late that his wife has fled to the bathroom and committed suicide by cutting her wrist in the bath. He is instead 'fascinated by the eyes of his enemy' (182). He 'seats himself before the bloody head set between the mirrors on the dresser and there gazes into its infinite deadness' (182).

'Blood and Water' is a story of inversions; two kinds of masculinity are pitted against one another: the rationalizing of the scientific establishment that cannot recognize its own monstrosity and the aristocratic masculinity of Sir Norman, with its propensity for madness. Defending his family honour by the use of the phallic 'tool', the latter metaphorically castrates the doctor, who, in an inversion of Lady Percy, also represents androgyny through the markers of the monstrous feminine on his body. Sir Norman's committal to Broadmoor does not prevent his resuming the role he had played so well all his life, that of the bucolic squire, and spending the rest of his life 'in a state of happy and imperious insanity' (183). McGrath pays tribute to one of the writers he most admires by using some lines of Melville's for Sir Norman's epitaph, which closes the story:

> What Cosmic jest or Anarch blunder
> The human integral clove asunder
> And shied the fractions through life's gate? (183)

The cloven 'human integral' may be a reference both to the division between the sexes and to the fragmentation of Sir Norman Percy's psyche, where the flanges (to use the plumbing metaphor) no longer hold.

The unfortunate doctor in 'Blood and Water' is not the only medical man to meet a gruesome end in the short stories. In 'The Skewer', it is again gendered identity and the potential uncanniness of the body that is instrumental in bringing about the demise of an all-too confident doctor. McGrath's interest in the gendered body reflects the fascination with gender instability in evidence in the popular culture of the 1980s. From Dustin Hoffman's performance in *Tootsie* (1982) to the popularity of Boy George and Divine's celebrated performance as a woman in *Hairspray* (1988), there was a growing awareness of the performativity of gender during this period. This awareness, that was to be so clearly articulated in theoretical work by scholars such as Judith Butler in the 1990s, became the stuff of a gleeful and often comic playfulness, in which parodic re-representations became of central importance. In a darker comic vein, Iain Banks's novel *The Wasp Factory* (1984) plays the kind of narrative trick with gender that is to be found in McGrath's story 'The Skewer', when its excessively masculinized narrator discovers himself to be biologically female.

In 'The Skewer', assumptions about gendered identity comically and literally cut down to size the founding fathers of psychoanalysis.[25] The all-too confident doctor in this story is evocatively named Dr Max Nordau,[26] and, it is implied, will have his eye put out with the eponymous skewer by the narrator. This will be in revenge for the torment he caused the narrator's uncle, who is revealed at the end of the story to be her/his aunt (the reader never learns the sex of the narrator). Neville (Evelyn) Pilkington's aesthetic and reclusive masculine identity, related to her disfigurement from an accident which killed her twin, has been a masquerade. The narrator states that her/his uncle's mind had taken 'a mystical, not to say Gothic, turn in the twilight of his life' (108). Nordau, however, claims at Neville's inquest that he had suffered self-inflicted torment: he had hanged himself in his London home, having already cut out his own eye in a Brussels hotel room. Neville's journal forms a significant part of the framed narrative and he writes of his harassment by visions of miniature psychoanalysts: Freud, Otto Rank and Ernest Jones and eventually 'the whole Weimar Congress', infesting his room like vermin (121). Descriptions of these encounters as they appear in the journal are interleaved with Nordau's report in the courtroom, giving an account of psychoanalysis as violence; it is the miniature Ernest Jones who uses a pen as a lance to put out Neville's eye, an act interpreted by Nordau as symbolic castration, in accordance with classic psychoanalytic theory. The narrator recognizes this as a 'phallocentric fallacy', although the reader does not discover Neville's biological identity until the twist at the end of the tale, which ends on a note of intended violent revenge: 'an eye for an eye, I say' (123). In the later novels, medical men continue to be represented as problematic characters, but the most suspect of all are the psychiatrists. In McGrath's most recent novel, *Trauma* (2008), the psychiatrist narrator is finally revealed to be himself deeply traumatized and in need of therapy.

In the American short stories, the doctor figure is notably absent. In contrast with this thematic figure, who, at this stage of McGrath's career, seems to be connected with his British past, creative protagonists are more in evidence: a painter, a writer and a photographer inhabit the pages of three of the stories. McGrath had left England after university and, following a spell in Canada, had been living in New York since 1981. Whereas the England of the short stories is that of earlier decades, an apocalyptic future and a distinctly Gothic late twentieth-century New York provide settings for several of the American stories. In another, 'Marmilion', there is a clear homage to the Southern Gothic tradition of Poe. In all of them, the Gothic concerns of transgression and decay remain paramount.

In contrast with the specific location and history which frame 'Marmilion', a ghastly future is imagined in two of the stories, reflecting the apocalyptic fears that many harboured in the America of the 1980s. McGrath has commented that as he was living in the United States during the Reagan era, he and many others found themselves speculating what the world would be like after a nuclear holocaust, when there were no human beings left to tell their own tale.[27] Neither of the first-person narrators of 'The E(rot)ic Potato' (his first published story) and 'The Boot's Tale' is human (being a fly and a boot, respectively). With their implication that human beings' ascendancy is inevitably doomed, both stories adopt a darkly comic treatment of the most abject subject-matter: corpses and cannibalism. In the case of 'The Boot', McGrath's story sits within a long tradition of satire, where an 'innocent' voice (in this case that of an inanimate narrator) lays bare the spiritual and moral bankruptcy of others. This story raises some uncomfortable questions about the positioning of the reader. Just as its human characters are lacking in human sympathy (a mother is eaten by her family without any compunction), their unsympathetic portrayal invites a similar lack of affect in the reader. Such a misanthropic vision is not, however, characteristic of McGrath's work. Some of his characters who commit abject acts, like Spider in the novel of the same name, tell their own stories; others, like Harry Peake in *Martha Peake*, are recuperated in the narrative. Always in the novels the human situation is rendered as complex, and this displacement of the human focus does not happen elsewhere in McGrath's fiction.

These two stories offer a blackly comic look into a bleak future; in the others, the past tends not to be far away in the present day. 'Marmilion', the homage to Poe, is set in a derelict mansion in the Deep South. Unusually for McGrath, the first-person narrator is a woman. She undergoes an uncanny experience and pieces together a speculative and possibly quite erroneous history for the house, its owners (the Belvederes) and the events that had taken place in the aftermath of the Civil War. Entering the ruined mansion, she feels 'something in the house react to [her] presence' but nevertheless spends the night there, only to be woken and terrified by the sound of something 'like a nail being scraped by a feeble hand against a brick'. 'Was there some sort of creature in the chimney?' she wonders; she has had 'the bizarre experience that something was trying to communicate' with her in the night (127). As a result of this experience she tries to find out about the history of the house and those who lived there. Her reflections on history anticipate the unreliability of historical narrative that is thematic in the 2000 novel *Martha Peake*; it is, she suggests:

> all a matter of *sympathetic imagination*. For to construct a cohesive and plausible chain of events from partial sources like letters and journals requires that numerous small links must be forged – sometimes from the most slender of clues – and each one demands an act of intuition. (134)

Her own partiality in the interpretation of events is there to read between the lines – a demand that McGrath frequently makes upon the reader. She is herself a Southerner, a 'monkey woman' – in other words, a photographer of monkeys. The story begins with an observation on spider monkeys that 'the Cajuns have long considered the spider monkey a great delicacy', adding, 'I should know: my husband was a Cajun' (126). Later in her narrative, she makes a strong statement about her alienation from the traditions of her own society, one 'dedicated to the greatest good for the smallest number. Endorsing such a society, I consider the moral equivalent of eating monkeys' (131). Her outright condemnation of the son of the family, William, is connected with her contempt for Creole society, which, she reminds the reader, has an aristocracy 'descended from thieves, prostitutes, and lunatics – Parisian scum forcibly recruited to populate the colony in the reign of Louis XIV' (139).

She has already speculated that no doubt the relationship between mother and son began to deteriorate at an early stage, and casually informs the reader, 'I should know; I've had a son of my own' (130). What emerges from her narrative is that her 'sympathetic imagination' may well be a projection of her own attitudes and familial failures. She feels close to the mother, Camille, 'like the wives of so many planters in the Old South, a deeply unhappy woman' (this, she adds, 'perhaps . . . accounts for my intuitive attraction to her') (129). When the historical sources can take her no further, she admits that the rest of the story is 'the construction of a sympathetic imagination' (140). She speculates that Caesar, Marmilion's former slave (who has fathered a child with the daughter, who died as a result of the birth), wreaks a dreadful vengeance on William for causing the death of Camille when she intervenes in his attempt to kill Caesar. The latter, she asserts, 'was a black nemesis, an agent of retributive justice'; he 'bricked him up in that pillar by the fireplace, buried him alive, upright and conscious' (141). In her desire to find out the truth of this speculation, she demolishes the pillar, to find instead 'the tiny, perfect skeleton – of a spider monkey' (143).

This climax to the story leaves an ambiguous closure, as the reader is left to reflect on the meaning of the nexus of identification between the narrator, Camille (whose historical trace, her handwriting, is described as 'spidery' (132)), and the spider monkey. As William Patrick Day suggests:

> The parody is above all the metamorphosis of one thing into another. It is, then, a literary device that perfectly embodies the mystery basic to the Gothic fantasy. Out of one thing comes two; the second subverts the first but is dependent upon it. While the parody subverts the original, it also affirms it, since it is a likeness of the original. The exact meaning of a parody, particularly in the Gothic, is always somewhat ambiguous.[28]

The motif of live burial, as suggested earlier, is recurrent in Gothic fiction; the discovery of the monkey suggests that the narrator's dream of nemesis is just that and that there is a chain of victimhood, which means that she has been the Gothic heroine all along. This story is an example of what could be termed 'simian Gothic', for monkeys and apes make an appearance in nineteenth-century Gothic texts from Poe's orangutan in 'The Murders of the Rue Morgue' onwards. Richard Davenport-Hines argues that there is a distinction between the simian fantasies of nineteenth-century writers like Sheridan LeFanu (whose malevolent spectral monkey in 'Green Tea' has resonances of not only subconscious urges but also the threat posed by the Irish poor) and of those in the twentieth century, like Karen Blixen. Blixen's story 'The Monkey' (included in her *Seven Gothic Tales*) makes the monkey a redemptive figure. In McGrath's tale, the monkey represents a perpetuated victimhood in which it is the narrator herself who is imprisoned by her history.

Whereas McGrath is able to draw on the long-established tradition of Southern Gothic in 'Marmilion', he adopts a distinctive approach to urban Gothic in his three New York tales. The concern with the Gothic aspects of embodiment in evidence in so many of the short stories appears here, too. As its title suggests, 'Hand of a Wanker' is a comic excursion into perverse sexuality; in it the Christian obsession with sexuality is rendered darkly comic through a jaunty and ironic narrative. Parodying the Book of Revelations, the 'beast' in this context is male sexual desire, represented by the severed hand, an image that echoes popular horror cinema.[29] As the title suggests, through its use of British slang, this story offers a comic take on a practice that caused the Victorians a good deal of anxiety and was a taboo subject in all but the coarsest company.[30] Characterized by the legendary hairy palm of the compulsive masturbator (in this instance the mark of the beast), the hand appears in a seedy nightclub in the East Village one late summer afternoon, where it proves itself to be as subversive and disruptive as its counterpart 'the Black Hand of the Raj'. In the final sentence, an indulgence in the florid writing of popular horror in the manner of H. P. Lovecraft, a reference to the 'putrid existential miasma that seethed within his guilt-ridden soul', is stopped short in a bathetic conclusion, as 'the stranger waved his stump over his head and limped off into the sharp Manhattan dawn'.[31]

Equally strange but less comic as a tale of Gothic embodiment and the decay of religion is 'The Angel'. 'I was very happy with that story,' McGrath told a recent interviewer:

> I was living on the Bowery at one stage and that's very much how I was experiencing New York at the time, sweating through those hot summers, couldn't afford to get out of the city, and there were all these curious creatures, men like The Angel – you saw Quentin Crisp every day on the streets.[32]

Identified by Andrew Hock-Soon Ng (who has written the only piece of sustained criticism on this story) as 'a narrative of the *fin de siècle* that is related to the crisis of representing the body',[33] 'The Angel' is marked by features that are characteristic of late nineteenth-century decadence. The city is represented as a place of corruption and decay in which the narrator, Bernard Finnegan, walks along a 'garbage-strewn and urine-pungent sidewalk' (1). The city as a locus of Gothic possibility is suggested by a 'rather grisly murder' where 'the body was mutilated and drained of all its blood', which leads the *New York Post* to suggest that a vampire may be on the loose' (5). The subject of Bernard's story, the old man Harry Talboys,[34] is one of the 'curious creatures' described by McGrath; he bears the markers of a late nineteenth-century dandy, the shabbiness of his clothes failing to disguise 'the quality and elegance of the cut' (1). His mouth is made up with lipstick and he habitually wears a 'fresh white lily' in his buttonhole, a flower associated with death. He is a subject waiting to be found by a dandified writer, Bernard, whose opening paragraph displays a self-conscious mannered excess:

> It was high summer when I met him, high summer in Manhattan, when liquid heat settles on the body of the city like an incubus, and one's whole activity devolves to a languid commerce of flesh and fluids, the ingestion and excretion of one by the other, and all sane organisms simply estivate. (1)

Bernard's narrative creates the frame for Harry's reminiscences as well as for a shorter intertext, in the form of a Gnostic tale that he discovers. In this, Satan, 'a great god', persuades a spirit called Arbal-Jesus to project himself into a human body, causing him great agony. Then, subjected to sexual abuse by Satan, his only consolation is the presence of another spirit in the body, that of Death. Along with this intertext, the *fin de siècle* markers in the contemporary New York setting point to the two dimensions of Gothic that provide the means through which Harry's story can be understood: the abhuman and the doppelgänger.

This is a story in the tradition of the abhuman, where the body and the city reflect each other in a state of deliquescent decay.[35] The angel of the title is revealed to be a body that cannot die but is condemned to live with its own putrefaction. Although Harry Talboys claims to tell the story of an acquaintance from the 1920s, in a classic Gothic doubling it turns that he himself is this 'Anson Havershaw', the darling of that emblem of frenzied modernity, the Jazz Age. Talboys, a figure of seedy and decayed splendour, 'liberally scented' and smelling 'like an old lady', but with 'a suggestion of overripeness in the bouquet' (2), is the late twentieth-century manifestation of Havershaw. The Anson Havershaw of Harry's account had claimed to be 'of the angels' and was a sexless and ethereal figure, whose body had only 'the merest suggestion of a navel' and was bereft of any identifiable genitals (8). Having dismissed Harry's story as the product of 'the gin fired fantasies of a maudlin old queen' (9), Bernard's moment of revelation comes when Harry displays his monstrous body to him, a body where the flesh is rotting away and the internal organs are visible through 'a thin strip of translucent plastic' (15). This is an uncanny body, in that, to quote Freud on Schelling, 'everything is *unheimlich* that ought to have remained secret and hidden but has come to light'.[36] It is a body that is both abjectly supernatural and pathetically human; instead of a flap of skin between his hipbones (his description of Havershaw's genital area), Harry has a 'tiny, uncircumcised penis', which is described as 'all puckered up and wrinkled in on itself' (15), an emblem of all-too human impotence beneath the impossibility of his decaying torso. The immortality of the Angel in this *fin de siècle* setting means being trapped in a mouldering human body without the prospect of death's relief.

The story's theme accentuates the uneasy relationship between Gothic and Christianity, and more specifically Gothic and Catholicism. Harry's apartment, with its vase full of lilies and its pervasive scent of incense, is like an extension of himself, redolent of a decayed Catholicism. As Bernard remarks, 'It reminded me of my childhood, of chapels and churches in which I had fidgeted through interminable Masses' (3). The aesthetic appeal of the Catholic Church, regarded by early Gothic writers like Radcliffe and Lewis as so treacherous, is part of Harry's past, and he tells of his affection for the old Gothic Revival church of St Ignatius Loyola on Park Avenue, which had been torn down in 1947. In the New York of the present day, Harry's angelic essence is forced to live on while his body is at one with the decay all around him. The secular cathedral of the Chrysler Building, an art deco monument to capitalism and modernity, is seen 'rising like a jewelled spearhead against the sky', while the crucifix on Harry's wall shines 'in the shadows of the fading day' (10). This is the fate of the angel in modernity. For Andrew Hock-Soon Ng, this abject figure of the angel is perhaps another version of the vampire trope; he suggests that Bernard's vampiric act as a writer, to draw on the lives of others, is turned in on itself as, 'like a vampire, Havershaw desires subsistence and replication through Bernard's writing so as to prolong his life-in-death'.[37] At the outset, Bernard states that he 'was a writer in those days', implying that he is one no longer. Thus, his encounter with the abhuman has robbed him of his artistic, writerly capacity; this suggests a deep anxiety about writing and particularly Gothic writing, for in representing the monster, one risks the danger of being consumed and obliterated by it.

The anxiety of the writer that is thematic in 'The Angel' also finds expression through the artist figure of 'Lush Triumphant', where the painter may be seen as an analogue for the writer. Jack Fin is a prototype for Jack Rathbone in the later novel *Port Mungo*. McGrath acknowledges that he has been able to draw upon a detailed knowledge of visual artists and their working practices through his relationship with a Bulgarian artist, the 'Orshi' to whom this collection of short stories is dedicated. The two Jacks and *Asylum*'s Edgar Stark are figures through whom the obsessions of the creative male are played out. 'Lush Triumphant' is memorable for its focus on the egocentricity of the artist and for the way it explores the uncanniness of artistic creation. As in 'The Angel', the squalor of 1980s New York is very much in evidence in this story. Set in the meat district of Manhattan, it provides a Gothic setting of the kind that was to

manifest itself in the tropical decay of Port Mungo in the novel of
the same name. This is 'a desolate and sinister place', appealing to Jack
because 'sinister desolation was his painterly *métier*' (43–4). It is an
abject place too, where a man might casually come across body parts
and 'inadvertently' kick 'a stray chipped liver' (47).

The plot concerns his artistic obsessiveness, which leads him to
disregard the last gasp of his failed marriage and to draw in some
obscure manner on the figure of a rent boy, with whom he is casually
but not in any active way sexually acquainted. This boy enters his
painting as an enigmatic hooded figure; Jack, however, does not
acknowledge the significance of this figure (described by the narrator
as 'the dark conspiring angel') that he has felt compelled to include,
as a 'ghostly herd' of 'hellish cattle' emerges on the canvas (51). A
Freudian approach to this story might read the finished picture as
a manifestation of Jack's id:

> he saw the bull very clearly: it was a beast with massive shoulders,
> heaving slabs of sheer muscle, and blazing eyes, galloping straight out
> of the yellow depths of hell, a thousand pounds of concentrated animal
> fury, timber-brown and oozing tar from every pore – now, that was
> power! (54–5)

Jack's conscious understanding of the painting is that it represents
his indestructibility, the fact that in spite of his self-destructive way
of life, he is 'a new type: built like a bull, incapable of suicide'; he is
'the lush triumphant' (51). He believes himself symbolically baptized
by his night-time drunken plunge into the Hudson, which he refers
to as 'baptism by filth' (49). At the tale's conclusion, once used for
the purposes of the artist, the boy has lost his mystery and is merely
a 'quite self-possessed cocky kid', unimpressed by the knowledge that
Jack is a painter (56). His shadow remains in the painting, however, an
avatar of death – a fact that is obliquely signalled by the final sentence
of the story, in which Jack 'thought he would call it *Beef on the Hoof*'
(56).

The short stories represent the earliest period of McGrath's career
as a writer. In various ways they demonstrate the qualities that led to
Richard Davenport-Hines's judgement that McGrath was 'a dandyish
stylist who depicts tumult, evil, monstrosity, disease, madness, horror

and death with hallucinatory menace'.[38] His strategy of playing with the established tropes of Gothic results in new representations of its enduring themes: transgression and decay. In the novels the three figures of the doctor, the artist and the mentally disturbed individual perform a complex textual dance, in which two of them are sometimes merged in one body and they are inflected by historical circumstance. McGrath's first novel, *The Grotesque*, constitutes a sustained exercise in impossible narration by a deranged mind, set, like a number of the stories, in a distorted but recognizable England of the recent past.

The Grotesque (1989)

Transgression and decay manifest themselves in various ways in *The Grotesque* (1989). Like the short stories, McGrath's first novel was written during the heyday of postmodernism and demonstrates a sophisticated layering of unreliable narration of the kind also seen in the work of such postmodern novelists as John Barth and John Fowles.[39] Once again, the chronotope is an England of the recent past, for McGrath a Gothic place, as the stories show. *The Grotesque* is set very precisely in the autumn and winter of 1949–50, on the cusp of a new half-century, a moment when many social changes were in train following the Second World War. The landed gentry, personified by Sir Hugo Coal (whose very name suggests fossilization), was susceptible as never before to the changes being brought about by increased social mobility, signalling the further erosion of a class system supported by a large body of servants. The physical location of the novel is identified as Berkshire, the county in which McGrath grew up, although this is a Berkshire modified for the purposes of the novel. As McGrath told one interviewer:

> I remember when I was writing *The Grotesque* I had the Berkshire marshes in there, and I'd been out of England for many years at that point and somebody pointed out to me that, in fact, there *are* no marshes in Berkshire – but by then it was too late. I *needed* there to be marshes and I wanted it to be Berkshire, for some reason, and so there it was: a completely non-existent landscape had sprung to life.[40]

The mapping of the landscape in *The Grotesque* through the use of names, however, signals the grotesque and parodic nature of the text. The nearest town to Sir Hugo's ancestral home is called Pock-on-the-Fling, hinting at disease tempered with the ludicrous (the ambiguous 'fling' possibly signifying the illicit sexual activity that takes place in the novel); the nearest village is Ceck, with the attendant Ceck's Marsh and Ceck's Bottom.[41] The house itself is named 'Crook', a name multiple in its connotations but suggesting here both deformity and criminality. McGrath's account of how he created the details of the house seems innocuous:

> I found a lovely little book in a second-hand bookstore in New York, called *The Manor Houses of England*, and I simply leafed through it, picking up details here and there – not only architectural details, but verbal details. The way that aspects of architecture are described – the sorts of terms that are used – can be as much a part of the creation of a building in fiction as a clear, purely visual picture in your mind. You catch a nice phrase that's used to describe, I don't know, a Jacobean staircase or a particular piece of detailing or masonry – and you fling it in because it sounds good, rather than just because it evokes a particular image.[42]

Yet Crook's solidity in the text also owes much to Poe, in the way in which, like the house of Roderick Usher, it is linked with Sir Hugo and his fate:

> Black against that darkling air, no line straight, it seemed a great, skirted creature that rose by sheer force of will to thrust its wavering gables at the sky – a foundering mastodon, it seemed, a dying mammoth, down on its knees but tossing its tusks against heaven in one last flourish of revolt. In the windows downstairs the lights shone into the night, and thus did the life of the house still burn, still feebly burn, and then, only then, as I stood at the bend in the drive and leaned, panting, after my climb, on my walking stick, only then did I experience a sudden intimation of mortality: my house would go down as I would go down; we were the last of the line.[43]

The monstrosity evoked in this description is part of a sustained pattern that reflects the title of the novel. *The Grotesque* takes its epigraph from Baudelaire: 'Nature is a temple in which living columns sometimes emit confused words. Man approaches it through forests of symbols, which observe him with familiar glances.' McGrath has commented elsewhere on the suitability of the epigraph: 'that particular idea of Baudelaire's was very appropriate to the grotesque with the ideas of biological breakdown, and the fusion between the biological, the animal, and the human which were very much at the centre of the book'.[44]

Such grotesquerie has both sinister and comic connotations. Wolfgang Kayser, in his influential book *The Grotesque in Art and Literature*, traces the evolution of the term 'grotesque' from its origins in the Italian *grotta* (meaning cave) to a term designating a

> specific ornamental style suggested by antiquity, understood [as] not only something playfully gay and carelessly fantastic, but also something ominous and sinister in the face of a world totally different from the familiar one – a world in which the realm of inanimate things is no longer separated from those of plants, animals, and human beings, and where the laws of statics, symmetry, and proportion are no longer valid.[45]

Sir Hugo, a self-styled gentleman naturalist, is identified not only with the house – here described as a struggling prehistoric creature – but also with the dinosaur bones he keeps out in the barn. These he vainly attempts to assemble into a creature he has named '*phlegmosaurus carbonensis*', the kinship with his own name creating an inescapable link between the two of them that signals his destiny. The process of decay and fossilization is, it seems, inescapable. The dinosaur's origin in Africa lends Sir Hugo's connection with it a hint of 'the unconscious, the unpredictable, the chaotic'.[46] Moreover, these are not the remains of a peaceable herbivore but those of a raptor; hence, Sir Hugo's identification with it suggests a propensity for violence which may be responsible for the murderous act that forms the core of the novel's plot. As McGrath suggested in a 1997 interview, the bones are an important theme in the book:

> Hugo's activity in reconstructing the bones of this dinosaur somewhat reflects his activity in putting together the various elements of reality, particularly concerning the events that have occurred in the recent

past in his house. There are suspicions that both are equally imperfect
... The dinosaur is also extinct, and Sir Hugo, as the social type of the
landed gentry just after World War II is another creature soon to
become extinct, and give way to a new man as represented by his new
butler, Fledge.[47]

The decay of the gentry in this novel is enacted through varieties
of transgression — social convention; sexual mores; the law of the land;
taboo; and fictional genre itself — making it difficult to categorize.
The novel situates itself in a variety of traditions and plays one off
against the other. This is a country house novel (drawing on that
tradition like 'Not Cricket' and 'Blood and Water'), a 'whodunnit' and
an eccentric novel of manners, as well as being a self-consciously
Gothic novel. A harmless and rather effete young man called Sidney
Giblet comes into the household as the prospective fiancé of Cleo,
Sir Hugo's daughter. At about the same time his wife, Lady Harriet,
employs a new butler, Fledge — and the inebriate Mrs Fledge. Lady
Harriet begins an affair with the sexually charismatic Fledge and
then Sidney mysteriously disappears. Eventually, after the persistence
of his mother who has come up from London, his bones are found
out on the marsh. His body appears to have been fed to pigs at the
pig farm attached to the Coals' estate. The Coals and their house
guests have eaten the meat from these pigs at a Christmas gathering
without realizing that they were, in effect, eating Sidney. The manager,
George Lecky, a faithful servant of Sir Hugo dating back to his African
days, is found guilty of Sidney's murder and hanged, but not before
accusing Sir Hugo of the crime at the last moment.

The novel is narrated by Sir Hugo; confined to his wheelchair,
following what may have been a cerebral haemorrhage in the course
of these events or may have been (as he claims) an assault by Fledge,
he has been pronounced cataleptic by a neurologist and deemed to
be 'ontologically dead' (16). Thus, its central premise is that the reader
has access to his mind, in which an apparently coherent narrative of
recent events — at least at first — is unfolded. The novel is narrated,
paradoxically, through the voice of an unspeaking subject but one,
the reader increasingly suspects, who is not a reliable narrator. No
other point of view but his is available, yet he admits to describing
events that he could not possibly have witnessed. He is as mute as

the dinosaur bones. From being master of the house, he has become passive watcher and listener, tended to by the drunken Mrs Fledge as if he were a baby. Paradoxically, for the reader, he retains total control over the story of what has happened in his household. In order to construct an alternative narrative, the reader must read against the grain and between the lines. His sardonic textual voice is seductive and gives language to a subjectivity that is detached, ontologically certain and, the reader comes to suspect, deluded. Believing himself to be ontologically very much alive, but condemned to 'vegetate for the rest of his days', Sir Hugo has come to the conclusion that he is destined 'to be a grotesque' (17).

The grotesquerie of the novel operates at a number of levels. In its physical manifestations it displays those qualities of abjection that characterize so much Gothic fiction, but it is abjection represented in such a way as to take it into the realms of comic Gothic.[48] The spectral, in the form of Sidney's ghost, as seen by Cleo, is of the rotting flesh variety: 'chalk-white, translucent, and tinged with a faintly greenish hue', with a 'great angry gash beneath his chin', 'he smelled unpleasantly sweet', she tells her father. She also adds some sartorial details: 'he was wearing the suit he'd been in the night he disappeared, a beige tweed affair, jacket and plus fours, with a faint check pattern in yellow and sky-blue' (164). The English country house is yet again shown to be an unsafe place for visitors, be they repulsive doctors, exotic-looking cricketers with possible vampiric tendencies – or merely mild young men with poetic tendencies and poor taste in clothes.

However, it is in relation to the boundary between animal and human that *The Grotesque* excels itself in grotesquerie and abjection. A guest at the Coals' table would have to share it with Sir Hugo's pet toad, 'Herbert' (named after his father-in-law). The toad has a history of appearances in Gothic fiction, most notably in *The Monk*, when the freed Agnes relates how 'sometimes [she] felt the bloated Toad, hideous and pampered with the poisonous vapours of the dungeon, dragging his loathsome length along [her] bosom'.[49] The sliminess of the toad gives it an abject aspect, which is accentuated in Sir Hugo's treatment of his pet as he treats him to a 'plateful of squirmy white maggots' at the dinner table. Sir Hugo's self-identification as a scientist underlies his belief that 'it's a mistake to pander to the squeamishness of women. Disease, infection, rot, filth, feces, maggots – they're all part of life's rich weft and woof'; his entertainment of Herbert at the table is intended to press home this point (15). The maggots, Sir Hugo informs the reader, come from the pig farm; the toad's reliance on the pig farm, therefore, introduces early in the novel the central motif of the pig.

Peter Stallybrass and Allon White's well-known analysis of the grotesque and the carnivalesque draws attention to the ambiguous relationship between human beings and the pig from the Middle Ages onwards. In the medieval fair and carnival, the pig occupied a focal symbolic place: both celebrated and used as scapegoat, it was admired for its qualities of usefulness while still being the object of disgust for its filthy habits. They also point out that, although within Christian discourse the pig was 'usually emblematic of definable sin, from the seventeenth century it became increasingly associated by the bourgeoisie with offences against good manners. The pig was demonized less for its supposed evils than for its rustic boorishness from which polite citizens must dissociate themselves.'[50] In the domestic context, they also point out, the pig often lived in close proximity to the family, transgressing the boundary between human and animal life that supports human identity. Such transgression is apparent in Sir Hugo, who, as the narrator of this story, is able to see and hear but not give any sign of consciousness, his appearance and behaviour being characterized by a 'compulsive grimace', 'grinding teeth', 'stertorous breathing', all of which are accompanied by, in the words of the doctor, 'guttural phonation not unlike the grunting of a pig' (16). Confined, grunting, to his wheelchair, Sir Hugo is cared for by Mrs Fledge, who undergoes a symbolic castration on his behalf when she accidentally chops off her finger in the kitchen. Bleeding helplessly, she sits drinking gin while Herbert laps away at the puddle of blood (179–80). Sir Hugo's vision of himself as 'a grotesque' means that he sees himself as a living example of what White and Stallybrass identify as a Bakhtinian definition of grotesquerie: 'the grotesque is formed through a process of hybridization or inmixing of binary opposites, particularly of high and low, such that there is a heterodox merging of elements usually perceived as incompatible, and this latter version of the grotesque unsettles any fixed binary-ism'.[51]

As Doris Fledge tends to Sir Hugo in his emasculated state, he harbours an intense hatred for her husband, while at some level identifying with him. Like Dr Jekyll with Mr Hyde, Sir Hugo comes to think of himself and Fledge as each other's double: 'I am his grotesque double', he says, 'he reads in me an outward sign of his own corruption' (173). Fledge and all that he represents is in the ascendancy, so that Sir Hugo sees himself relegated to an abject state in what had been his own domain: 'just as the gargoyle on a Gothic church was a defeated demon forced to serve as a sewer, so, inversely, am I forced to serve as a gargoyle in this anti-cathedral, this hell-hall that Fledge has made of Crook' (173).

McGrath cites Joseph Losey's *The Servant* (1963) as an influence on the novel.[52] Losey's film offers a darkly ironic look at the British class system in a story involving an upper-class bachelor and a contemptuous manservant, who assumes authority over his 'master'. Sir Hugo recognizes that Fledge 'is not a born butler' (11), having reflected that 'butlers . . . are born, not made; the qualities of a good butler – deference, capability, a sort of dignified servility – are qualities of character that arise in cultures where a stable social hierarchy has existed, essentially undisturbed, for centuries' (11). After Sir Hugo's 'cerebral accident', Fledge takes to wearing his master's clothes and aping the manner of the English country gentleman. Thus, he comes to occupy Sir Hugo's place at the centre of Crook, regardless of Sir Hugo's judgement that 'a change of costume did not transform him . . . into a gentleman' and that he lacks 'something essential . . . a certain facial creasing that would denote affable scepticism and the expectation of deference' (152). It is no coincidence that Fledge and his wife have also been in Africa; appointed by Lady Coal, they 'had been in the employ of a coffee planter in Kenya who apparently was trampled to death by an ox', hence a lack of references. Thus, as in the short stories, Africa acts a signifier for the uncontrollable; in the case of Fledge, it is also associated with Sir Hugo's unspeakable desires.

Sir Hugo's obsession with Fledge's usurpation of his role colours his version of events at Crook. Fledge's transgressions, his rapacious sexuality and potential capacity for violence, can only be read through Sir Hugo's account of them, an account that, as discussed earlier, is not only unreliable but, coming from one deemed to be 'ontologically dead', impossible. His belief that he has seen Fledge and Sidney in an embrace arouses his class prejudices: in determining who bears the major responsibility for the encounter he weighs Fledge's greater years against Sidney's superior social class. This incident needs to be viewed in the context of his erotic dream from the night before that he recounts. He had dreamt of Mrs Fledge, transformed into a provocative sexual figure bearing markers of both genders: she is wearing her uniform with stockings and suspenders; she is also wearing men's underpants ('oddly enough, like my own', says Sir Hugo) and has a 'curiously deep voice', and she turns her back to him; 'she offered me her bottom' (50–1). At the culmination of this wet dream, Fledge appears and, he says, 'I sat up in bed with a shout' (51). This suggestion of repressed desire for Fledge himself signals the transgression of not only sexual norms but social ones, too. A victim of what Eve Kosofsky Sedgwick has named 'homosexual panic',[53] Sir Hugo projects his urges on to another, while continuing to desire the male body. When he fantasizes about sexual encounters between Fledge and Lady Harriet, it is Fledge's naked body that is described in intimate detail as the object of desire, with 'its fine penis rising stiff and faintly throbbing from that soft fleece of red-brown pubic hair' (169).

Sir Hugo's ambivalence towards Fledge reflects fears of both social and sexual transgression. Sir Hugo may have killed Sidney because of homosexual jealousy; the disposal of his body by feeding it to the pigs leads to an act of cannibalism (albeit once-removed), a taboo involving transgression of a more fundamental kind. In the grotesque violation of boundaries that patterns the novel, food mingles with both sex and death. Sir Hugo envisages Fledge seducing Harriet for the first time in the larder, in a characteristic moment of comic incongruity: 'But now she looks up into his face, and there between the pickled gherkins and the rhubarb chutney a rather warm, liquid event occurs inside her' (77). Sidney enters the food chain, to be consumed, once-removed, in the ham and pork from Crook's pig farm. The ham is used for sandwiches at a Christmas reception for the local Roman Catholic community, of which Harriet is a stalwart. Sir Hugo enjoys some 'light eschatological chat' with the local priest, in which he draws attention to the cannibalistic ritual that is normalized in the Roman Catholic Church, the belief in transubstantiation (83). The explanatory discourse of psychoanalysis fares badly in the novel, too, represented as it is by Sir Hugo's nephew, with the lewdly punning name Victor Horn. 'A fat boy' who plans to be a psycho-analyst when he grows up, Victor has brought a copy of Freud's *Totem and Taboo* with him as Christmas reading. The uncanny is given short shrift by the precocious Victor, who, on hearing an outburst from Cleo about a 'hideous, stinking, evil thing . . . crawling around outside this house', says to his father, 'Daddy . . . I think that's hysteria, but I'm not sure what sort' (96). Meanwhile, as Sir Hugo reflects, 'We had all, indirectly and unknowingly, eaten Sidney' (162).

Ultimately, Sidney's fate is no different from that of the dinosaur in the barn, no different from that of all of us: to become bones. All that remains of Sidney is found out on the marsh, in the form of gnawed bones. The dismembered dinosaur is multiply significant. It is judged to have been violent and carnivorous, both features echoing the events at Crook; its close association with Sir Hugo suggests that he may have had more to do with Sidney's violent end than his own narrative acknowledges. Sir Hugo has spent much of his time out in the barn trying to assemble the bones in the right order, but some are missing, and there are doubts as to whether he has put things in the right place. This is an obvious analogy with his narrative; both are unreliable. It is implied, however, that this is not simply Sir Hugo's problem: the dinosaur is the focus of a quasi-empiricism that tends to make claims for scientific truth but is based on speculation. It may, indeed, be an image for Sir Hugo himself, spurned by the professional scientific community and already an anachronism in the post-war world, just as his house is likened to a prehistoric beast. As Sir Hugo moulders in his wheelchair, the dinosaur bones become covered in fungus and he dreams that he is growing into the chair, 'in the process of turning into a sort of giant plant', and has a vision of how he would 'merge organically with Crook' (157). The novel achieves closure, however, with a transcendent vision of the wrongly executed George ascending from the garden with 'a sort of silvery radiance . . . spilling forth' (186). As in 'Blood and Water', aristocratic insanity is tinged with visions of the sublime.

Three of McGrath's novels have been adapted for the screen; the earliest of these adaptations was *The Grotesque*, in 1995. Its original title was *Grave Indiscretions*; it reverted to *The Grotesque* and then became *Gentlemen Don't Eat Poets* for its American release. Its changes of title are a sure indicator that, in spite of some well-known star names (most notably Sting as Fledge and Alan Bates as Sir Hugo) it was, in fact, a 'turkey', neither commercially successful nor lauded as an art-house movie. The *Los Angeles Times* said, 'Beyond its athletic lovemaking, *Gentlemen Don't Eat Poets* plays like a cheap homage to "Alfred Hitchcock Presents". It telegraphs its punchlines well in advance and has exhausted its wit by the final anticlimactic note.'[54] Although McGrath wrote the screenplay, he was not happy with the resulting film, describing it in a 2005 interview as 'a bit of a muddle'. 'They laid it on thick', he added.[55] In the attempt at what could be described, using the framework suggested by Linda Cahir, as a literal adaptation, a more two-dimensional text is created and the complex layers of narration are lost.[56]

The film adaptation instead adopts a linear narrative, dealing with the challenge of the first-person narration by intermittent voice-over. Sir Hugo's stroke is not shown until nearly the end of the film. This means that the audience is invited to take certain events on trust, in a way that the novel's reader is not. Its erotic scenes, for example, are given a validity as *mise en scène*, which the novel never allows because of the constant reminders that Sir Hugo's version of events is un-reliable and that he is projecting his desires and fears on to other members of the household, particularly the enigmatic and self-seeking Fledge. The sexual ambiguity sustained through Sir Hugo's novelistic narrative is resolved in the film into clear pointers to his own repressed homosexuality and into scenes of sexual encounter, the authenticity of which is not questioned. The film does not throw into doubt the claim that Fledge is the seducer of Sidney as well as Harriet, but instead reinforces his self-serving sexuality. Scenes are also inserted to indicate Sir Hugo's inclination towards violence, such as his acting out of his dinosaur's predatory character in the pub, only just stopping short of disembowelling the resident tomcat.

The choice of exterior settings of the film, on the other hand, eschews the Gothicism of McGrath's narration, in which the very names are grotesque. Whereas in the novel 'Crook' lives up to its name, the imposing and elegant Norfolk stately home, Heydon Hall, is used for Sir Hugo's ancestral house. What the film lacks in exterior setting it makes up for in interior shots, however; often at odd angles, they are embellished by Gothic accessories – Sir Hugo taking a bath with a python coiling sinuously overhead, for example.

The comic aspects of McGrath's novel are lost in the dream sequences (Mrs Fledge's men's underpants have disappeared) and in the representation of Sidney's ghost as he appears to Cleo, in the novel a mixture of the spectral and Bertie Wooster. There is a toning down of some aspects of the grotesquerie of the novel, too, particularly in the case of Mrs Giblet, Sidney's mother, who is a grotesque caricature of Dickensian aspect:

> her throat swung bagged and cross-hatched from a wrinkled knob of chin flanked by rouged jowls loosely depending from lumpy cheekbones. Powerful gusts of stale air emanated from the crannies of her person; the little dog was curled in her lap like a hairy tumour. (65)

In the film she appears merely imperious; in this instance, 'laid it on thick' does not apply. Herbert, however, has a starring role, which opens with Lady Harriet picking maggots from a dead hedgehog for his supper and, in a plot change, ends with Cleo extracting his venom in order to poison Fledge, whom she believes to have killed Sidney. The film omits the scene in which Mrs Fledge chops off her finger in the kitchen and Herbert drinks her blood; although it seems to focus on the abject aspects of Gothicism, it is reticent when it comes to body horror. In one respect the visual medium is very effective, however: the appearance of Sir Hugo and Fledge in identical clothes creates an uncanny doubling effect; this visual representation of the shift in the balance of power offers only a hint of the deeper social changes which the novel suggests will overtake the dinosaurs of this post-war world.

The Grotesque marks the end of the earliest phase of McGrath's fiction. In these works, there is a fertile re-imagining of the persistent Gothic concerns of transgression and decay through a parodic engagement with the 'mannered' features of earlier Gothic works. In this early fiction, the past is indeed a foreign country and the reader's guidebook is disturbingly unreliable. Black comedy is the tone of most of the stories, and this dark humour is sustained throughout *The Grotesque*. The comedic tone creates a distancing effect, so that in spite of the prevalence of first-person narrators, empathy is not the primary affect. McGrath was to exploit the fictive potential of first-person narration in his next three novels, each of which offers in its own way a complex and disturbing representation of madness.

2

The Transgressive Self

❧❧

The three novels of the 1990s – *Spider* (1990), *Dr Haggard's Disease* (1993) and *Asylum* (1996), all set in mid twentieth-century Britain – move away from the playful pastiche of the earlier work. If the waning of affect believed by Fredric Jameson to be one of the characteristics of postmodernism is evident in the short stories and in *The Grotesque*, this is not true of the novels of the 1990s. Their Gothicism lies in the way they represent the unstable boundary between the sound mind and madness. McGrath draws on his father's tales from Broadmoor and his own experiences of mental health care in Canada to create convincing representations of shades of madness. Poe's legacy is again evident in the world of tortured psyches of these novels, in which the transgression of social norms and the destabilization of the boundaries of the self drive the narrative. Madness in McGrath's work is always manifested corporeally, the permeability of the boundaries of self often manifesting itself in unstable bodies and a context in which entropy is always immanent. The narrative mode of the novels invites an empathetic identification which results in the reader becoming complicit in judging where those boundaries lie. The texts are formally complex, their unreliable first-person narratives full of false clues and semantic echoes. Instead of the playful parody of Gothic conventions that characterizes the earlier works, they emanate a brooding Gothic atmosphere in a past that is recent, yet remote from contemporary experience. However, rather than representing a departure from the grotesque, they may be seen as developing the tendency further. As Christine Ferguson suggests, this narrative practice is itself aligned to McGrath's fascination with the grotesque:

> Stylistically, in placing conventional authoritative narratives in the mouths of conventional and unreliable narrators, and thematically, in constructing the madman as both alien and familiar, his literature belongs firmly to the realm of the grotesque. In the paradoxes and contradictions of his discourse, we find a mordant glee in the failings of taxonomic classifications and the futility of all attempts to establish an objective, orthodox version of reality.[1]

These narrators are located in settings that do more than provide background: they root the novels' characters in behaviour and attitudes characteristic of the time. Furthermore, the medical discourses that permeate them are located at a particular point in history and have an ambiguous relationship with the Gothicism of the texts. The eponymous Spider has, the reader learns in the course of the novel, been a patient (or inmate) in a secure psychiatric hospital. He is released into the community by doctors who are themselves deluded into thinking he now believes in his responsibility for the events leading to his incarceration. The novel is structured around the journal he begins to keep, in which he attempts to tell the true story as he remembers it. In using Spider's as the narrative voice of the novel, McGrath faces the challenge of representing a confused and deluded mind without descending into textual incoherence. As readers are drawn into the web of the narrative, the threshold beyond which they begin to doubt its veracity depends upon a conscious act of interpretation; they are in danger of being drawn into Spider's madness.

The two later novels' first-person narrators are both doctors. Initially, they seem to speak with the voice of reason, yet in both these cases that threshold is there for the reader, too. Whereas Spider appears outwardly odd (and therefore possibly mad),[2] the same cannot be said for Dr Cleave, in *Asylum*, or, at first, for Dr Haggard. Edward Haggard claims to have discovered a new disease, which he projects on to the son of his dead lover. In his vanity and delusion, he thinks it could be named after him. The title of the novel is ambiguous, in that, as his narrative progresses, the reader will realize that it is Haggard himself who is diseased. The case of Peter Cleave is more subtle; he tells a story of multiple transgressions that ostensibly locates madness in two other characters, not in its rational and apparently dispassionate psychiatrist narrator. All three novels invite the reader to make a judgement about where s/he stands on the spectrum of mental soundness. As Scott Brewster has pointed out, 'in identifying irrationality or pathological disturbance in Gothic writing, we admit, even succumb, to the strange "logic" of fictive madness'. Can we, he asks, 'since critical interpretation involves readerly desires . . . recognize and diagnose "textual" madness without implicating our own delusions and anxieties?'[3] Sander L. Gilman's work on disease and representation has this to say about perceptions of madness:

> The banality of mental illness comes into conflict with our need to have the mad be identifiable, different from ourselves. Our shock is that they are really just like us. This moment, when we say 'they are just like us', is most upsetting. Then we no longer know where lies the line that divides our normal, reliable world, a world that minimizes our fears, from that world in which lurks the fearful, the terrifying and the aggressive.[4]

These novels represent the 'New Gothic', according to McGrath and Morrow's own definition. Death, decay and transgression are the hallmarks of all of them; madness, as Foucault has commented, is the '*déjà là* of death'.[5] Although characterized by qualities of Gothic excess, their complex formal qualities point to a subtle parodic effect, a postmodern parody that is, to repeat Linda Hutcheon's words, 'repetition with critical difference'.[6] Their fractured narratives present texts that are writerly rather than readerly in Barthes's sense of the terms; reading these novels is a Gothic experience.

Spider (1990)

McGrath's account of the genesis of *Spider*, as explained in an address to the Annual Meeting of the Royal College of Psychiatrists in 2001, gives an indication of a creative process that resists the telling of a plain tale:

It was a novel I had begun with a simple premise: a plumber in the East End of London murders his wife, buries her in the potato patch in his allotment and moves a prostitute into the house in her place. Various complications arise, but basically this was a simple sardonic tale about a murdering plumber, or so I thought. It was when I had settled on the plumber's son as the narrator of the story, who in adulthood remembers those desperately unhappy days of his boyhood, that I came up against the real challenge. It occurred to me that the man remembering the circumstances surrounding the death of his mother was remembering it wrong: his memories were a set of elaborate delusions. Such a possibility was intriguing, but then in answering the questions of why and how this could have come about, I realized that my narrator had schizophrenia.[7]

Readers of 'Blood and Water' might already be inclined to ask why McGrath had initially chosen a murderous plumber as the focus of the novel and to speculate that the internal logic in this simple narrative might already suggest some darker subtext. Once the decision had been made about the narrator, however, the fundamental premise of the novel changed. The challenge was to represent credibly the workings of a schizophrenic mind. As McGrath has commented:

It became . . . very much a technical problem of keeping this whole mindset of symptomatic terrors, delusions, obsessions, fixations and so on, so I constructed a delusional system to do with gas, gasworks, bits of string and rope and webs, and slowly put together the elements in the process of having him tell his story.[8]

The web is the structuring metaphor in *Spider*, the narrator spinning a narrative that can trap the reader. This is not the social web of the realist novel;[9] this is, rather, the web that is the contradictory and distressing reality of Dennis Cleg or, as he thinks of himself, 'Spider', a nickname his mother had given him. Rendering it was a technical challenge for McGrath, as he has explained in a recent interview:

I wasn't feeling his pain so much as I was working hard to render his confusion with as much plausibility as I could, and yet ensuring that it remained comprehensible to the reader, so that the reader wasn't thrown back in despair at having to confront Spider's chaos. And that really was a technical rather than an emotional ordeal.[10]

If the reader is to create a coherent narrative from the iterations and semantic echoes in Spider's confused narration, an act of interpretative closure is required. This cannot happen, however, until the reader has entered into the tortured labyrinth of his mind and ventured with him into traumas of his past. In a sense, the novel demands that the reader engage in an act of psychoanalysis. Some of the stock images from Freudian psychoanalysis are there, most prominently a loathing of the father and a vexed Oedipal relationship with the mother. It becomes apparent, however, by the end of the novel that psychiatry has failed Dennis Cleg; deemed fit for the outside world, he is cast out into 'the community' and begins to keep a journal so as, he says, 'to create some order in the jumble of memories that the city constantly arouses in me'.[11]

This attempt at the creation of a coherent narrative is counterpointed by the web-like linguistic structure that contains the clues to an alternative narrative, one other than that uppermost in Spider's conscious mind, which becomes increasingly confused as the novel goes on. This is paralleled by his sense of physical disintegration. Not only does he believe that a smell of gas is emanating from his body (the significance of which becomes gradually apparent), but as he descends into incoherence, he believes that he has become 'an anatomical monstrosity', in which his alimentary tract has been inverted so that his anus is now at the top of his head, one of his lungs has disappeared and the other is inhabited by a worm (175–6).

The novel is set in the docklands of the East End of London, both in the 1950s (the present day of the novel) and the 1930s of Spider's childhood.[12] In the present day of the 1950s, he is living in a bleak hostel, a kind of halfway house run by a Mrs Wilkinson. In the tale he starts to tell, 'Canada' is his signifier for absence – a faraway place to which he believes his father claimed to have sent his mother. He also identifies it as the place of his own exile, which as his story progresses he acknowledges as the similar-sounding 'Ganderhill'.[13] His account of this asylum suggests that it is a place in which he had found some degree of peace in 'the good years' (181), truly an asylum from his troubled past. One of the few memories of happiness he has is that of tending the vegetable gardens there, under skies that were 'blue, with white clouds moving across in stately caravan', when, he says, his 'spirit exulted' (174).

In contrast, the East End is a grim place. With this setting, McGrath exploits an already textualized Gothic geography and adapts it for the pathology of his disturbed protagonist. Spider's London is T. S. Eliot's 'unreal city', a waste land with its own 'dull canal' and 'gas house'. For the contemporary reader, this part of the East End is a place of urban regeneration, where the historical docklands have been transformed into the financial centre of London and the world. The labyrinthine streets and persistent fog of the earlier twentieth-century East End of *Spider*, however, are evocative of the urban Gothic of Victorian fiction, the fictional world of Robert Louis Stevenson's *The Strange Case of Dr Jekyll and Mr Hyde* (1886), for example. As Robert Mighall and others have demonstrated, the ruined castles and abbeys of the earlier period of Gothic fiction were replaced in the nineteenth century by different threatening environments.[14] Mighall notes how in Dickens's work, for example, 'certain parts of London, despite their distance from the castles and monasteries of the Radcliffian landscape, are rendered as strange and remote in their own way as these more traditional Gothic locales'; Dickens, he claims, adopts a mode of writing which 'defamiliarizes and distances that which it purports to reveal'.[15] The persistent fog has a realist dimension, being a wellknown characteristic of the London cityscape for many years before the Clean Air Acts of the 1960s, but its presence in the novel also echoes Dickens's pervading metaphor in *Bleak House*. The constant reference to it in Spider's narrative of the events of twenty years before suggests that it signifies confusion in perception, as, for example, in Conrad's 1902 novel *Heart of Darkness*. It is in *Heart of Darkness* that Conrad's Marlowe reminds his audience on a ship moored in the Thames Estuary that this, too, has been one of the dark places of the earth.

Although Spider describes the grim post-war landscape of the East End in Orwellian detail, it has for him a spectral quality: 'There was blackened brickwork, and grimy walls, and against them grey figures in raincoats hurried home like phantoms through late winter afternoons before the lamps were lit' (12). Its haunting power is more personal than this, however; it is a landscape freighted with personal memories that he cannot at first decode or that he chooses not to divulge. The gasworks, most notably, hold sinister but un-acknowledged connotations for him and he tries to avoid looking at them. 'Gas' is uttered repeatedly through his narrative; the smell is pervasive, and some of the first warning signs of the distortion of his perception are his observation that the gas seems to be 'seeping from my groin' and his claim that 'they don't have gasworks in Canada' (30). Here McGrath offers a new twist on the nineteenth-century urban Gothic's distinctive emphasis on the olfactory. As Robert Mighall has noted:

> In general the early Gothic romances were not conspicuous for their attention to smells . . . The horrors of the first Gothic novels were principally associated with sight and touch . . . Within a hundred years Gothic fiction has become more fastidious about smell . . . stench could itself become a Gothic property and evoke its own horrors.[16]

For Spider, the smell of gas is associated with an as yet unidentified horror.

Yet this is an urban landscape in which the river and the purifying presence of water are also perpetually present. The constant reference to rain (also characteristic British weather) and Spider's liking for it in the later period suggest the desire for cleansing and possibly rebirth in water. Water is a constant motif, in a novel set beside the Thames; it is a marker, too, of the unattainable. In McGrath's own words, 'He is dying of thirst in a world of wet.'[17] The river and the canal both set boundaries to Spider's world. Set against the images of water are those related to houses, both the hostel run by Mrs Wilkinson and Spider's childhood home. In the latter, the very walls are impreg-nated with horrors, as the 'night-hag' lurks in the damp walls. The cellar is a place of horror in which Spider recalls being beaten by his father, Horace. The Spider of the 1950s is accommodated at the top of the old house that serves as a hostel, immediately beneath the attic. The attic here is also rendered as a Gothic space in the tradition of, for example, Charlotte Brontë and Charlotte Perkins Gilman. Spider is increasingly tormented by sounds coming from overhead that he believes to be demons or imps. It is also, the novel suggests, the scene of Spider's death, as he purposefully hides the rope he has found.

Spider's boyhood home is central to the narrative of his past. This East End terrace is the Gothic house, the keeper of secrets and place of unspeakable horror; the home of the family which harbours dangers, its structures at one and the same time regulating and focusing desire. When Spider begins to remember his childhood, in the second chapter, he takes the reader beyond the squalor of his descriptions of his current surroundings. His memories of the bedrooms evoke for the reader an earlier Gothic narrative of madness, Charlotte Perkins Gilman's much-quoted short story, 'The Yellow Wallpaper':

> the bedrooms had been wallpapered so many years before that the paper was moist and peeling, and badly discoloured in patches; the large spreading stains, with their smell of mildewed plaster (I can smell it now!) formed weird figures on the fading floral pattern and stimulated in my childish imagination many fantastic terrors. (16)

His nightmares had frequently figured an 'awful humpbacked night-hag . . . a spirit damned for her sins against men' (24); this manifestation of the female grotesque is later to be translated into the sexualized figure of 'Hilda Wilkinson', the prostitute whom he believes has replaced his mother. As in Gilman's tale, the boundary between inside and outside is for Spider terrifyingly blurred, so that when he says of the London of his boyhood, 'it was a clotted web of dark compartments and narrow passageways' (13), it could be his own mind he is describing.

As he delves back into his childhood memories, he explains why the name 'Spider' had been given to him by his mother, an affectionate name derived from her happy memories of a country childhood which she relates to him in 'a mood of lyric tenderness', describing 'the fresh cobwebs glistening in the elms at sunrise' (42). As a boy, he had fallen into the habit of adopting the identity of Spider when negotiation with the outside world had become too much to bear. 'Spider' became an identity that he had kept in the back of his head in what he describes as his 'two-head system'. While the bad boy Dennis was being flogged by his father in the cellar, Spider was 'upstairs in his bedroom' (98). Thus, the central character of McGrath's novel is shaped by the discourse of disassociation now familiar to contemporary readers as typical of the victims of abuse. He also represents the doubling familiar in Gothic fiction from Hogg's *The Private Memoirs and Confessions of a Justified Sinner* (1824) onwards. As Lucie Armitt has commented: 'The narrative is full of uncanny doubles, as Spider's confused mind superimposes living and dead characters, one upon another, in tandem with which chronotopes continually shift and blur.'[18]

This childhood doubling is there for the reader to decode in the narrative of the adult Dennis. The Spider of the novel's present is a monstrous figure with 'long spidery fingers . . . stained a dark yellow round the tips . . . the nails . . . hard and yellowy and hornlike' (13). At the extreme of his sense of bodily transformation, he believes himself to be 'playing host to a colony of spiders', an '*egg-bag*', as he sees himself urinate 'tiny black spiders' from 'a small pipe-like apparatus, something from a plumber's toolbox', a description that not only indicates his alienation from his body, but intimates to the reader the inescapability of and revulsion at an identification with the father (176–7). He perceives his present life as a kind of limbo, his fellow boarders as 'passive, apathetic creatures, dead souls' (10). His decision to keep a journal gives shape to his narrative that is the substance of the novel; the Spider of the present weaves a web of memories. Referring often to himself in the third person, he constructs an initially coherent but false narrative from his fragmented memory, which then begins to disintegrate. For the reader there is a trail of clues that this narrative is unreliable, and an alternative narrative is uppermost by the end of the novel.

He tells a story of an abusive father who murders his long-suffering mother and replaces her with a prostitute, Hilda, whom 'Spider' in his turn murders by gassing her in the kitchen. This can also be understood as the fantasy of a mentally disturbed child, probably the victim of domestic violence at the hands of his father, for whom puberty involves the unpalatable recognition of his mother as a sexual being. She becomes for him uncanny and monstrous. In order to come to terms with this, he creates an alter ego for her in the shape of Hilda, an abject figure, a 'monstrous feminine', to use Barbara Creed's term.[19] Hilda's bodily functions are foregrounded in Spider's account of her. She belches, farts, drinks and has sex with his father; her corporeality becomes over-determined as he alludes to her pervasive smell (87) and physical functions. Indeed, he describes her at one point as 'some large female animal' (82). His obsession with her physicality is re-counted in some detail in his journal, to the extent that he recalls that 'when Hilda went to the Ladies I climbed on a barrel to see her pee' (196). Given the persona of a prostitute, Hilda is 'the woman I'd seen in bed with my father' (89) as he had observed them having sex, 'groaning as one creature as the creaks and screams of the old night-machine settled into a rhythm that affected the watching young Spider strangely' (83). His own pubertal sexuality emerges in mastur-batory references as he describes having 'a wank in the outhouse' (102), a memory which recalls his earlier account of Hilda masturbating his father by the canal, and the description of his father's penis as being 'unusually thin' and 'stiff as a pencil', a strange image that alludes to the activity of writing, through which he is conjuring the scene (40).

Hilda has taken over his mother's role and, wearing her clothes (according to Spider's account), her identity. The idealized mother figure (who haunts his memory while he is at Ganderhill) is slight, contained and spectral: 'that small slim figure in coat and headscarf, clutching her handbag and standing, say, in the dappled shade of the elm tree by the wall' (180). He projects the Hilda persona on to his landlady in the contemporary narrative and wonders at the co-incidence of their sharing the same surname, whereas it becomes apparent to the reader that he has appropriated her surname for the persona he has projected on to his mother. He recalls her words of greeting and believes he now understands their significance: '"We've been expecting you," she might have said, "so we can finish the job we started in Kitchener Street, twenty years ago"' (201).

Although Spider represents his father as an oppressive Gothic figure (his very name, Horace, evoking the name of the widely acknow-ledged father of Gothic itself, Horace Walpole), father and son are linked in the midst of the urban environment by gardening and growing. Horace's retreat from Kitchener Street is his allotment, the working-man's access to his peasant roots, 'a sanctuary, a sort of spiritual haven' as Spider describes it. At this early point in the novel, he is telling the reader that he had spent years abroad, where he had become 'something of a gardener' himself (18). As in the short stories 'The Lost Explorer' and 'The Arnold Crombeck Story' and in *Asylum*, the garden is an ambiguous image, reflecting the unstable relationship between culture and nature. Spider's early reflections on Horace and his allotment are sympathetic. 'In a very real sense', he tells the reader, 'the allotment was the spiritual core and flavour of a life that was otherwise loveless, monotonous, and gray' (19). As he writes his journal, however, this sympathetic identification evaporates. The allotment becomes the site of his mother's murder and her burial beneath his prized potato plants (78). Later, with Hilda established in the house, Spider describes how he cuts into a potato at dinner and sees it ooze blood, in one of a series of accumulated clues to the unreliability of his murder narrative (117). The manure heap at the allotment is a reminder of the inevitable decay of all things organic. Eventually acknowledging that Canada is actually the asylum Ganderhill, Spider comments 'better you smell grass than gas' (139). Here, he finds the spiritual sanctuary he had understood his father's allotment to be, and he is deprived of this by his release and return to the unsympathetic streets of East London. His final memories before the suicide that is implied at the end of the novel is of lettuce, of Augustas, 'the sweetest and most buttery', but central to this memory is his discovery of the lost false teeth of a violent patient, lodged in the heart of a lettuce. This is a garden despoiled by human anguish and a memory fraught with a dark humour for Spider: he had thought he heard the lettuce echo the voice of the teeth's owner and say: 'Where are my brains, you bastard!' (221).

For Spider, the act of writing gives coherence to a set of fragmented stories, but the textual nature of that coherence irrupts into the narrative (for example, when he compares his father's penis with a pencil (40)), and its unreliability is thus foregrounded for the reader. Indeed, Spider himself tells of his sense of 'being written' as he writes, a sensation that arouses in him 'stirrings of terror' (134); for he is 'conscious always of the danger of shattering' (135). There are linguistic echoes and reverberations throughout the text, creating a multi-layered effect. 'Horace', for example, not only evokes Walpole but is close in sound to 'horrors'. The challenge to the reader is to recreate a rational and 'true' narrative by interpreting the clues dotted throughout Spider's own account of his history. However, his delusions are seductive and immerse the reader in the world as he sees it. There is also an invitation to empathy as the reader is invited to experience the world through Spider's eyes. He has 'progressed' in Ganderhill by going through the charade of acknowledging his crime and showing remorse for it, but in his account this is not what he believes. The false acknowledgement of his crime has permitted his release, as his doctors deem him well enough to be released, but the return to the streets of his childhood will lead to an irrevocable disintegration.

Through writing his journal he comes to see the new superintendent in Ganderhill as his father, referring to him as Cleg-Jebb. Threatened with being discharged (because 'I need your bed' (187)), he had attempted suicide. When confronted by Dr Jebb with the challenge to admit responsibility for killing his mother, he had shouted back, 'You did!' (190). The journal tells a different but disintegrating story, and it is only at the end of the novel that he eventually encounters a different truth from the one he has been relating to the reader. Whereas the mother has become forever inaccessible, transmuted into the protean form of Hilda or the spectral vision at Ganderhill, he comes to internalize the murderous Gothic father he has made of Horace. Returning to Kitchener Street, to the pub (the Dog and Beggar), he feels himself merging with his father's identity: 'I had been appropriated, I felt, dragooned, impressed, and I watched in futile rage as he behaved in his old ways' (215). Moreover, now believing that his landlady is Hilda Wilkinson, he, as his father, watches her 'hungrily from shifty furtive eyes that always slid away when she became aware of him' (215).

Engaging with effort the landlord of the pub (the evocatively named Ernie Ratcliff) in conversation, he is told that Horace Cleg had died in the war, killed by the bomb that had obliterated the family home. It is Ernie who performs the function of truth-teller in Spider's first-person narrative, revealing that Horace had already been 'destroyed' by the death of his 'missus', whose 'boy turned the gas on' (216). His acknowledgement of this alternative narrative of the death of his mother is represented through a brief section of third-person narrative, in which he recalls the events of the day when 'Hilda' died and how he laughed while she was 'loaded onto a stretcher and covered with a sheet', at the same time being 'puzzled' and sensing 'dimly . . . that some sort of mistake had occurred' (218). There is nothing left for Spider after this but to contemplate killing himself. He resumes his journal and, addressing the reader in an intimate tone, begins to plan his suicide, rejecting the cleansing embrace of the river in favour of death by hanging in the attic. Rather than leave only 'a dirty book stuffed up a chimney' (an echo of the earlier story 'The Smell'), he will kill himself where the demons, 'those bloody creatures of hers', can see what he has done (219).

Spider has generated interest in psychiatric journals, where Dennis is regarded as a subject for analysis. Writing in *Advances in Psychiatric Treatment* in 2004 Femi Oyebode judges the novel to be: 'a study of the architecture of psychotic experience. The struts and girders upon which illusions, hallucinations and delusions are built are exposed. It is also a study of the mundane everyday life of an individual with chronic psychosis living in the community.'[20] In a review of the three novels considered in this chapter, Harold Carmel suggests that *Spider* (1990), is 'a brilliant portrayal of the inner world of a person suffering from schizophrenia', displaying 'a [*sic*] immense array of psychotic experiences, from hearing the chattering of imps in the attic to feeling his innards shrivel. By the end of the story, the reader, initially believing Spider's account, becomes aware of how Capgras syndrome has complicated the picture.'[21] The tendency of the professionals to focus on the pathological, however, means that other aspects of the novel are neglected. Dennis, it is suggested, displays the behaviour of someone suffering from a syndrome that involves failing to recognize close family members, believing them to be imposters.[22] As the central figure of a fictional narrative, however, his role in the text has more complex implications than this would indicate.

Literary critics have found that McGrath's novel invites psycho-analytic readings. Magali Falco focuses on the biographical underpin-ning of the novel, suggesting that the novel contains a coded message to the novelist's father, Dr Pat McGrath, and is hence a personal text 'qui comporte entre ses lignes un message caché que le lecteur se doit décrypter – un message codifié qui était d'abord destiné au Dr McGrath' ('that carries between its lines a hidden message that the reader must decipher – a coded message that was meant in the first place for Dr McGrath').[23] According to McGrath, however, he valued the advice of his father in relation to the credible creation of Spider:

When I produced the schizophrenic, Spider, I spoke to my father who was very complimentary and said it was the best fictional account of a schizophrenic he had encountered. But when I explained how I thought the book would end, with Spider getting out alive and glimpsing that his entire structure of memory had been unreal, my father shook his head. He said 'that is not what happens to men like that'. It was a darker vision than I had in mind, but he spoke as one who knew.[24]

Adopting a different approach from Falco's, Lucie Armitt suggests that while 'it is tempting to read *Spider* as a straightforward oedipal narrative' (in which Spider harbours violent fantasies about his father, but 'is also clearly in love with his mother'), there is also another way of interpreting the novel. She bases her reading on Abraham and Torok's concept of cryptonomy, which is concerned with transgenerational haunting. As Armitt sees it, the child Dennis is drawn into the mother's web and invited to share her secrets: 'sitting in the kitchen knitting while she tells her tale, this mother, is, quite simply, the spider in question, wrapping Spider up in an elaborate but seemingly flawless narrative while weaving the reader in as well'.[25] The adult Spider's journal that reworks the narrative fabrication is, in a classic trope of cryptonomy, hidden up the chimney. Armitt points out that Abraham and Torok identify the topography of the crypt as 'an enclave . . . sealing up the semi-permeable walls of the dynamic Unconscious', and sees Spider at his bedroom window representing their positioning of the ego, which is 'given the task of cemetery guard . . . When it lets in some curious . . . detectives it takes care to serve them with false leads and fake graves.'[26]

Armitt's persuasive analysis also notes that *Spider* is 'concerned with the conflict between private and public and inner and outer worlds' and points to the wartime location and the choice of the name of 'Kitchener Street'.[27] Gothic has always been about history and histories, and a vexed relationship with the past is one of its characteristics; the Orwellian rendition of the area in McGrath's text evokes a twentieth- century history that is characterized by squalor and violence. McGrath's urban Gothic here performs what Robert Mighall has claimed for Peter Ackroyd's London fiction: it performs a 'séance; for the city's dark voices'.[28] In the very names, there is an echo of the violence of history itself; the name 'Kitchener Street' indeed evokes the ill-fated militarism of the First World War, and Spider says that 'Kitchener Street was blackly contaminated long before any of these events occurred, every brick of the place oozed time and evil' (92). In this broader historical sense, the Cleg house is Gothicized, its very architecture redolent of levels of violence. The violent father-figure was himself obliterated by a greater violence when the house was wiped out by a direct hit from a German bomb in the Second World War, a traumatic period of London history that has otherwise passed Spider by during his long stay in Ganderhill. The East End to which Spider returns is disorientating: 'the Slates', a warren of streets, has disappeared and in its place is a bomb-site. Spider's internal world may be nightmarish, but there is scant comfort to be found in the world outside. When he finds the courage to return to the place of his childhood traumas, he finds only a void, created by the violence of the outer world from which he was long shielded in the asylum.

Spider's ejection from Ganderhill seems callous, but also suggests that, if his bed is needed, his malaise is more prevalent than one might think. As in all McGrath's work, the representation of the medical profession is less than sympathetic. The old superintendent, Dr Austin Marshall, does no more than pass the time of day by talking about naval battles and riding, but his regime is benign. His successor is a more modern man, who displays no empathy at all and who sends Spider out into 'the community'. (It is perhaps no accident that the doctor who supervises Spider in the community is called McNaughten, in an echo of the McNaughton Rules, which define the terms under which someone cannot be held criminally responsible by virtue of insanity.) Spider's experience reflects a process that had been under way since the 1960s and was accelerated by the policies of the Thatcher government in the 1980s, which involved the closing down of many large mental hospitals and the ejection of their inmates into what was euphemistically called 'the community'. As McGrath has commented, 'Those big Victorian loony bins at least gave people shelter from a world they found alien and threatening – unlike care in the community where de-institutionalized people are left wandering the streets with no care at all.'[29] In returning to the environs of his childhood, Spider returns to reconstruct his past. This is clearly a Gothicized past; in the same way, the novel, while not acknowledged by its author as Gothic, is haunted by its Gothic antecedents.

The complexity of McGrath's novel is thrown into relief when it is compared with David Cronenberg's screen adaptation (2002). Cronenberg's film engages with the uncanny at the heart of the novel in powerful visual ways, and through the collaboration between novelist/screenwriter and director something new is created. Given Cronenberg's reputation for body horror, his treatment of McGrath's novel is remarkable. The original text gives ample opportunity to present scenes of Gothic horror by showing the more 'florid' of Spider's schizophrenic hallucinations: his intestines 'pulled to the back of [his] body and twisted about [his] spine . . . like a snake' (140) or his memory of finding a baby with a hole in the top of its head 'and through the hole I sucked up and swallowed everything in the baby's head until its face collapsed like an empty rubber mask' (196). Cronenberg rejects all of this, however, in favour of a pared-down symbolic landscape, creating a film that is poetic, poignant and even elegiac, rather than monstrous. Whereas the novel achieves a technical feat by rendering Spider's schizophrenic perspective through a complex linguistic web, which echoes the central metaphor of the book, the film boldly adopts a different way of telling his story.

Very early in the film-making process, Cronenberg and McGrath agreed to abandon any notion of the voice-over. Spider's voice in the film is reduced to largely incoherent mutterings; his physical presence, however, remains throughout. The opening of the film shows the audience his oddness, as 'ordinary' people get off a train in a London terminus and he, the very last to emerge, is left alone on the platform, conspicuously 'odd'. Economically, therefore, the film not only sets up the action – Spider (played by Ralph Fiennes) appears immediately as someone bound up in his own world.

The textualized Gothic space of Spider's childhood East End becomes in Cronenberg's film (both in the present time of the film, which seems to be the late 1980s, and in the 1950s of Spider's childhood) a place of preternaturally empty streets, in which Spider wanders alone in an uncanny limbo. The web of memory that he has created for himself appears in the film in various visual metaphors: string that he ties around his attic room in the hostel, a broken mirror pieced together again in the hospital in one of the key flashbacks, and the structure of struts surrounding the gas cylinder that has a looming surrealistic presence in the narrow streets. Spider's preoccupation with gas is shown both by this powerful symbol and the acting out of his belief that he can smell it coming from his own body. It is thus removed from the device of the journal, which appears in close-up as an indecipherable patchwork of text. Spider's belief that his father had murdered his mother and replaced her with a prostitute is also acted out in the film; the adult Spider is present in all of these scenes, 'watching' as he remembers. The device of using the same actress, Miranda Richardson, to portray the mother, the prostitute and, eventually, the warden of the halfway house, replaces the linguistic clues of the novel to the unreliability of this narrative. By the end, the multiple significance of the web has become fully apparent to the audience.

This successful adaptation avoids a literal translation to the screen, eschewing body horror in favour of an exploitation of film's capacity to render the uncanny visually and dramatically. Spider's final en-counter with the identity of the woman he murdered is acted out in the film when he sees the woman lying dead in his father's arms outside the family home change from Hilda the prostitute to his mother. McGrath's engagement with Gothic is always self-reflexive; what Cronenberg's film succeeds in doing is presenting the unstable frames of identity and perception that characterize his narratives and constitute his 'New Gothic'. *Spider* draws its audience into a chilling encounter with the *unheimlich* at the heart of a family narrative. In achieving cinematic success, however, the film loses several dimen-sions of the novel. Its engagement with the abject, as the very bound-aries of Spider's physical identity become unstable, is deliberately muted, so that the 'powers of horror' engendered by the 'florid hallucinations' are not invoked. Most significantly, the very precise historical and geographical location of the novel is lost, making the film less multidimensional than the novel. The East End of the novel is a far more abject place than that of the film; Spider's hallucinations are framed within an environment which is already brutalized and squalid. McGrath's text engages with history itself; Spider encounters a literal void in Kitchener Street, one created by the communal mad-ness of war and the mass death of the Blitz. His years in Ganderhill provide sanctuary not only from his tortured past but from the large-scale violence of the public world. This is an image McGrath was to return to in 'Julius', the middle tale in his trilogy of stories about New York, *Ghost Town* (2005): spending twenty years in an asylum in the Hudson Valley, Julius misses the American Civil War.

Spider represents a significant development in McGrath's fiction. Although the intertextual echoes of other Gothic fiction remain, these are much more muted than they are in the playful parody of the early stories or the gruesome black comedy of *The Grotesque*. In following the Poe-inspired influence to look inward and to represent 'transgressive tendencies and extreme distortions of perception and affect',[30] he succeeds in creating a work of complexity and subtlety. Spider's story is, however, inseparable from its urban Gothic setting; this is a personal history embedded in a public history that is redolent of its own horrors. In the next novel, *Dr Haggard's Disease*, the relationship between private and public transgression becomes even more marked. In its protagonist, the medical man and the madman become one and the same; in a time of national crisis, rational discourse and the authority represented by the doctor are put under intolerable strain, as what begins as a story of lost love is transformed into a Gothic tale of multiple transgression.

Dr Haggard's Disease (1993)

Louis A. Sass identifies 'the poles around which images of madness have revolved for so many centuries':

> on the one hand, notions of emptiness, of defect and decrepitude, of blindness and even of death itself; on the other, ideas of plenitude, energy and irrepressible vitality – a surfeit of passion or fury bursting through all boundaries of reason or constraint.[31]

Foucault, in *Madness and Civilization*, observes that 'It is true that long before the eighteenth century ... passion and madness were kept in close relation to one another' and explains how passion may be subsumed by madness:

> Madness, which finds its first possibility in the phenomenon of passion, and in the deployment of that double causality which, starting from passion itself, radiates both toward the body and toward the soul, is

at the same time a suspension of passion, breach of causality, dissolution of the elements of this unity. Madness participates both in the necessity of passion and in the anarchy of what, released by this very passion, transcends it and ultimately contests all it implies.[32]

McGrath's third novel (described by one reviewer as 'one of the finest modern novels yet written about thwarted passion'[33]) has, like *Spider*, a tightly controlled and complex narrative structure. It turns out to be a quintessentially Gothic tale, one told from beyond the grave and thus breaching the most fundamental of boundaries, that between life and death. This becomes clear to the reader only at the very end of the novel as the narrative is interrupted mid-sentence when death takes the narrator. It is only then that the outer frame of this complex framed narrative comes into complete focus: the 'you' of the narrative is James, the son of Edward Haggard's deceased lover. Haggard's voice, throughout the novel, is addressing James as he lies dead in the shadow of his burning plane. There is also an implicit address to the reader, as Haggard's version of events unfolds and his state of mind reveals itself. His voice is characterized by competing discourses and switches between three narratives nested inside one another. The outer frame is taking place over a short period, as a crashed plane burns on an airfield. The narrative beneath this places Haggard in the period he has spent as a general practitioner on the south coast, following a crippling accident and the loss of his married lover. The interior narrative is the story of that love affair in the London of the late 1930s, where Haggard had been working as a junior doctor.[34] The narration is seductive for the reader: whereas in *Spider* there are early clues to incoherence in Spider's observations and memories, Haggard's discourse seems for much of the time entirely rational and characterized by an assumed authority, conferred by his status as a doctor.

His account of his love affair with Fanny, wife of the senior pathologist Ratcliff Vaughan, is tinged with nostalgic detail, the 'smoky quality' of the air (3) at one with the 'smoky velvet' of his lover's voice (20), the London fog and ubiquitous cigarette smoke misting the picture. Against this background, Fanny appears as a shimmer of silver, with her 'silver-plated lighter' (2) and, more intimately, her 'silvery silk drawers' (91). Compared with a background world peopled by

Piker-Smiths, she is represented as an exotic creature, her dubious political sympathies for Hitler pushed to one side by Haggard, in the grip of an overwhelming infatuation, but her dangerous qualities intimated by such details as her 'closely fitted, dark-green, turbanlike hat jabbed with a parrot's feather' (39). His life is bounded by the harsh institutional environment of the hospital and his shabby bedsitting-room, which Fanny transforms with expensive items for her own comfort. There is a glimpse of the pampered luxury to which she is accustomed when Haggard visits her home; 'I can't give you any tea, I'm afraid ... Iris has gone shopping', she tells him, in her 'drawing room with aquamarine curtains, silk-shaded lamps, and richly patterned rugs on a gleaming wood floor' (135). Once she is seen in this setting, the reader recognizes exactly why she has no intention of leaving her formalin-scented husband for a life of relative poverty with a junior doctor. 'Go away – get on with your life – get on with someone else', she tells him (137). Vaughan's discovery of their affair, however, leads him to take a jealous revenge by throwing Haggard down the hospital stairs. This results in his becoming crippled and addicted to morphine; his account of his experiences of pain and addiction veers between rational medical discourse ('you open it up, dissect away the muscle, and bang in a steel pin' (120)) and Gothic delirium, in which he is tormented by 'grotesque dreams' where Vaughan has him on the dissecting table (130).

The novel explores the relationship between madness, delirium and passion. Although at the level of plot it concerns the aftermath of a doomed love affair, its dominant theme is transgression at several levels: adultery; betrayal; violence; drug addiction. The medical man looks for scientific explanation and is sceptical about that which cannot be proved; the lover in the throes of his affair with the wife of a senior colleague speaks the language of passion and transcendence; the disappointed lover and ruined doctor of the outer frame has become a morphine addict, trapped in a liminal space in which he claims scientific judgement but shows himself to be increasingly deluded. He comes to believe that love has transcended scientific limits and returned Fanny to him through the transmutation of her son's body into hers. He is a 'phantom of the man who first glimpsed [James's] mother in a north London church' (4); near the end of the novel, the Gothic figure he has become is thrown into relief as he describes himself on the beach wearing a woman's cast-off fur coat he has acquired because it reminds him of Fanny's: 'I walked on the beach, I stumped up and down in my fur, raging in my distraught mind against the prospect of the darkness to come' (175).[35] He occupies a Gothic space, marked by Gothic signs, in which landscape takes on a symbolic significance and buildings are imbued with a threatening sense of identity that can sometimes appear as agency.

The outer narrative, the present time of the novel, is set on the south coast of England in 1940, during the Battle of Britain. Both time and place are significant. (Haggard's last meeting with Fanny had taken place on 'the day Hitler entered Prague' (134).) At this point in history, this coastline was the front line, under assault from German planes and in constant need of defence. As a border continually under threat it is an outward and visible sign of the other kinds of vulnerable boundaries in the novel. James, Fanny's son, is a Royal Air Force fighter pilot stationed near to the coastal town where Haggard has taken up general practice. He is a man broken in body and spirit, dependent on daily fixes of morphine to get through the day. Following the end of his affair with Fanny and his serious injury at the hands of her husband, he had bought his house and practice in the autumn of 1938. This act had involved a retreat into what appears to be a Gothic fortress; early in the novel, he describes in great detail his first view of the Victorian house, Elgin,[36] set high on the cliffs above the town, and its effect on him. He 'gazed in dawning wonder at its steeply gabled roofs, its tall chimneys, its many windows, each one high and narrow, with lancet arches and slender leaded frames' (7). Bearing an air of Gothic decay ('an air of neglect, of decrepitude, almost, clung to the place' (7)), it is sited perilously near 'the edge of a cliff that dropped a sheer hundred feet to black rocks and churning sea' (7). In spite of these ominous markers, Haggard describes it as 'a romantic house, a profoundly romantic house', suggestive of 'the restlessness of a wild and changeful heart' (7). Taking up residence, he 'haunted it with her memory' (7). He initially ignores the more sinister Gothic associations of the house, although he presents the retiring doctor as a Gothic figure ('His head was deathly pale and almost hairless' (8)). It is only halfway through the novel that he recounts an incident from a Christmas visit to his uncle, when he had first seen Elgin. His uncle had told him how a nearby church had finally been swept into the sea by a great storm which had exposed a new face of the cliff, in which 'could quite clearly be made out the forms of human skeletons' (84). In this powerful image of a breached boundary, the skeletons are an uncanny reminder of the proximity of death as the novel uses Gothic tropes to represent Haggard's condition. He has been drawn to a Gothic place, near this decayed and desanctified church where 'an atmosphere of melancholy desolation' had grown up and 'there were reports of unearthly forms flitting among the ruins' (84).

In this space, the boundary between life and death becomes unstable. Haggard's desire to keep his beloved with him by cherishing her memory takes a sinister turn. As in *Spider*, the reader is drawn into the mind of the narrator and his delusion so that s/he must decide at what point rationality has deserted Haggard. In the course of his confessional narrative, he relates how he had admonished himself with the voice of the doctor:

> Oh, what are you doing? I asked myself. Isn't there something ridiculous about all this – you feed your obsession with the woman with morphia until you're unable to think of anything else, you can't sleep, you can't even stay in the house – as though Elgin were your own head, your own mind. (61–2)

This he says after an experience when he feels himself to have entered 'an unknown and possibly dangerous region', in which 'the cliff face felt alive, alien, hostile – benevolent watchers by day, those bulwarks, now they were monsters, living gargoyles' (61). He had already acknowledged that his mind might have played tricks on him in making the house come alive in a grotesque manner. He tells of the night when he thought he had seen 'some small movement in the *wall*' and describes the pattern of cracks as forming distinct patterns:

> the longer I gazed into the wall, following the intertwining, convoluted lines of the patterns, and identifying newer and stranger grotesques half-hidden in its frenzied sweeps and swirls, the greater became my feeling of unease and excitement – the cracks in the plaster were no mere accidents of time, but *the product of conscious design*. (25)

For the reader who has read *Spider*, this Gothic image may be understood as portending madness.

'Trust me. I'm a doctor', although a cliché, is never a maxim to adopt in reading McGrath's fiction. In the world of his novels, doctors are never represented in a good light. At best they are avuncular and unfocused, like the superintendent at Ganderhill; at worst, arrogant, self-interested and tending towards the physically monstrous, such as Cadwallader in 'Blood and Water'. Ratcliff Vaughan (whose propensity for violence is demonstrated by his treatment of Haggard) falls into the latter category. The medical profession is as much a product of modernity as is Gothic, and the two are often connected because of their respective concerns with death and the body. Ratcliff reminds young Haggard that 'It's the *pathos* that conditions the *logos*'; in other words, as he elaborates, 'life . . . can only create a science of itself by means of dysfunction and pain' (77). 'Ratty' Vaughan is a pathologist who smells of formalin ('the smell of death' (77)) and has run to fat, with 'a roll of pink flesh at the collar' (3). He is represented as being intimate with death: he is 'a bare-hands man' who scorns the use of rubber gloves while he dissects (109). Even while she complains that 'he [comes] to her smelling of death' (74), his status and relative wealth allow him to possess the exquisite Fanny, and she allows herself to be possessed. His name suggests an allusion to Ann Radcliffe's fiction, in which the patriarchal house incarcerates the Gothic heroine. Complicit in her own oppression, Fanny may be seen as being in thrall to death itself.

McGrath's late twentieth-century novel invites the reader to consider the inadequacies of the profession in its earlier state, thus undermining its mastering discourse. The doctor from whom Haggard buys his practice has been in the habit of prescribing a placebo, 'mist explo', on the grounds that the body has 'an immense capacity to heal itself', but 'it's got to be persuaded'. Initially dismissing this as 'mumbo jumbo' (28), Haggard finds himself beginning to take the same approach. Worse, putting physical symptoms down to psychological causes, he misdiagnoses his solicitor's wife and, believing her symptoms to be hysterical, decides she should be admitted to a private asylum; she subsequently dies, having lost all confidence in the medical profession: 'I was later told by the superintendent of the asylum that she had for some time before her death refused to see a doctor, claiming that none of us knew what was wrong with her' (147). Haggard's account of his life as a surgical registrar in the London hospital St Basil's is given substance through a wealth of realist detail. However, St Basil's is also represented as a Gothic space. Haggard's mentor is Vincent Cushing, so named, according to McGrath, as an allusion to the famous surgeon, Harvey Cushing, but inevitably, for a reader versed in twentieth-century horror film, recalling two of its most famous actors.[37] This is perhaps a case of unacknowledged textual haunting. Haggard describes Cushing as 'a tough, bloody-minded character' ('like your father', he tells James) who 'treated surgery like a branch of mechanics' (17). While Haggard's account has something of the quality of A. J. Cronin's fiction of the period[38] in its stories of struggling young doctors – a masculine culture in which there is no room for the faint-hearted – he does not flatter himself. His history at St Basil's is undistinguished at best and at worst negligent. 'I'd begun to realize I wasn't meant to be a surgeon', he admits (16). Distracted, he is even worse, leaving a fingertip from a rubber glove in a patient and struggling to perform a spinal tap.

In *Dr Haggard's Disease*, passion and the madness attendant upon it are enacted through the discourse of the body. The boundaries of the body are unstable for Haggard; the transcendence of self promised by sexual passion (both thrilling and threatening) becomes translated into the abject. As Kristeva explains, 'The abject is edged with the sublime. It is not the same moment on the journey, but the same subject and speech that brings them into being'.[39] Fanny's abrupt dismissal of her lover is a betrayal of the language of Keatsian romanticism through which they had conducted their affair; Haggard, on the other hand, clings to it. He tells James that love for him is not ephemeral, not 'a flight into madness or ecstasy', but 'an exalted or sacred condition'. 'For what is sex after all but a cleaving together and a fusion?' muses Haggard.

> It is the making of the two into one, the recovery of a lost unity . . .
> it is a Platonic idea . . . She completed me but I lost her. And having
> known fusion and wholeness it became impossible to live without it
> – I'd rather *never have known* that such a condition was possible. (63)

It is the nurturing of the lost love affair, whereby Haggard pledges to 'make it an object of worship and construct an altar in my heart where I could perform, nightly, my devotions' (64), that moves him into a state of Gothic abjection.

For in this novel, such intersubjective encounters are acted out at the corporeal level. The body becomes the battleground for identity – from the lyrical romantic discourse of the lover to the abject vampiric trace in the final kiss given by Haggard to James. External events, such as the invasion of Europe and the Battle of Britain, are analogous with this more personal battle. As Haggard realizes he has lost Fanny he fantasizes, hobbling on his crutches, that armies marching across Europe are marching to the same chant that he is repeating in his head: 'You have to let her go' (126); he learns of her death just after the declaration of war (138). His own body is irrevocably invaded. The pain from his badly healed injured hip becomes personified in the form of 'Spike', a 'familiar' of sorts and an enduring reminder of the intervention of the dominant father-figure, Vaughan. Perhaps even more intrusively, morphine makes its demands on his body, so that he is in thrall to a different master from the delirium of passion. As Haggard's mental state deteriorates, images of dismemberment enter the text. There is nothing of the comic in these images (as in the earlier fiction); they irrupt into the text in ways that suggest the disintegration of perception. Fanny's body manifests itself to him unexpectedly but in a fragmented way: 'One morning I was examining an old man with a lung condition ... when suddenly I saw your mother's wrist' (65). In his dream of the destruction of Elgin by a German bomb, he finds himself holding his housekeeper's shoe (a traditional Freudian symbol) and remembering Fanny's 'delicate foot' (172). This is a dream that ends with the vision of an angel in the shape of James, her son.

It is James's body that becomes the ultimate battleground in this war. A Battle of Britain pilot, one of the legendary 'few', he is destined to lose his life at the hands of both an enemy fighter (which has caused his plane to crash) and Dr Haggard, who cannot bear to see him 'too badly burnt to live' and has killed him with an overdose of morphine to save him suffering (179). His relationship with James becomes increasingly complex. From the outset, he has been struck by the young man's likeness to his mother; 'You even sounded like her', he says, remembering their first meeting. He becomes increasingly obsessed with him and the resemblance he bears to Fanny. Through his bravery as a pilot he sees him as the object of romantic adoration: 'You were knights of the air; and you, dear James, were *my* knight, my gentle, parfit knight, you were one of that brave doomed breed sick with nostalgia for something worth fighting for, something worth dying for —' (151–2).

When James's shrapnel injury introduces a sliver of metal into his body, in a phallic echo of 'Spike', Haggard has cause to treat him, reflecting that his skin is like his mother's. At this point he believes he observes an irregularity in James's body. In a reversal of Lady Percy's bodily transformation in 'Blood and Water', there is – or so Haggard believes – evidence of feminizing changes: 'there appeared to be something peculiar about your penis' (156) and (here adopting the scientific discourse of the doctor) 'imperceptible, perhaps, to any but the trained medical eye, mild gynaecomastia with slight enlargement of the nipple' (157). Coming to believe that shock – the trauma of modern warfare – is responsible for a new syndrome relating to the pituitary gland, he envisages making a case study of James that would lead to the recognition of a new disease, egotistically named 'Haggard's disease' (161). When he tells James that he is sick, the latter replies, 'Not me, doctor . . . you' (160). Believing in James's progressive feminization, he transfers his romantic desire to the son, who now bears the traces of silver ('I . . . saw you in my mind's eye at the bar in the mess, a scrap of silver silk knotted about your throat' (177)): 'I felt a distinct movement of sexual feeling towards you' (176). These homosexual yearnings are readily recognized as such by the other pilots, who, in tune with the homophobia of the time, mock him.

The climax of the novel locates sickness in Dr Haggard himself as his delusion comes to full fruition. As James lies seriously wounded, Haggard believes that his dead mother has entered his 'ruined dying body': 'I press my mouth gently to yours and probe for your tongue with my own, probe with tiny darting flickers till I taste in your terrible burnt head the fresh sweet wetness of the living tongue within —' (180). In this moment, the vampiric nature of Haggard's relationship with James becomes apparent. This has already been tinged with an implicit necrophilia, through Haggard's earlier reflection that James's presence 'in the hills above this moribund seaside town . . . seemed to [him] . . . like a whisper of dark necromancy, as though spirit were somehow being breathed into a corpse' (76). This final abject act, however, parallels the invasion of James's body by the death-dealing injection, itself an echo of 'Spike', and demonstrates the 'perverse and predatory sexuality' of the vampire.[40] The final unfinished sentence of the novel signals the ultimate coalescence of death as, it implies, the plane explodes, engulfing both of them in flames. The climax of the novel is thus both an act of extreme abjection and an act of transcendence, as Haggard believes at the moment before death that he has been reunited with Fanny. As a tale told from beyond the grave, it is confirmed as Gothic in its ultimate transgression.

Asylum (1996)

The third novel in this group has its primary setting in another version of *Spider*'s 'Ganderhill', a secure psychiatric hospital where Stella, the enigmatic wife of the new deputy superintendent, embarks upon an affair with a charismatic inmate, an artist who has murdered his wife.[41] When he absconds, she follows him, with ultimately disastrous results. Although transgression and decay characterize Stella's life story, the novel's dominant theme is that of possession, the desire to transgress the boundaries of another person. Stella's story is told by a psychiatrist at the hospital who, it becomes apparent, is far from disinterested; as his narrative unfolds, he demonstrates that he is a stranger to passion but intimates a sinister desire for control. Dr Peter Cleave is very different from the tormented Dr Haggard, yet his manipulation of the stories of Stella Raphael and Edgar Stark, his artist patient, eventually appears to be as transgressive as Haggard's final embrace of the dying James. An ageing bachelor, he lives alone in a 'handsome house a few miles away with its fine paintings, its fine furniture, and its fine library', a 'measured existence'.[42] The reader is entirely dependent on the narrative of Cleave (who shares a name with the vampiric character in 'Not Cricket') for knowledge of Stella. The dispassionate tone of the narration seems to distance the novel from the Gothic, and the drab late 1950s setting is rendered in detail. Although Cleave's narrative voice resists a Gothic tone, emphasising instead the empiricism of the doctor, the novel's concerns are undeniably Gothic and it is shaped around a powerful symbolic structure relating to boundaries. Without boundaries, there is no transgression. Like *Dr Haggard's Disease, Asylum* renders the boundary between passion and delirium unstable, while yet again drawing attention to the instability of the category of madness itself. The passion of art and the incipient madness of the artist becomes one of the central themes in this novel. It also calls into question the boundaries imposed by gender and class expectations; as Cleave reflects, the first time Stella has sex with Edgar was 'what shifted her beyond the law, not just the criminal law but the law of her marriage, her family, and her society, which of course was the hospital' (78).

Asylum's themes are themes already familiar in McGrath's fiction. The figure of the artist, first seen in the short story 'Lush Triumphant', is given further substance in the character of Edgar Stark. Varieties of madness are thematic here, too, manifesting themselves in different kinds of transgression and decay. Psychiatry as a rational and mastering discourse is called into question, and eventually the reader is forced to ask disturbing questions about the relationship between the psychiatrist and his patients. Cleave controls Stella's story throughout the novel, dropping hints and clues and only gradually divulging what he knows. It becomes apparent as the novel progresses that he has pieced together her story partly from his own observations and partly from what she has told him, in what becomes a relationship between doctor and patient. The intimate detail of many of his descriptions of scenes in Stella's life, although giving substance to the narrative, can only be a product of his imagination. His desire for possession is ultimately parallel to that of Edgar, although in the case of the latter it is manifested in murderous jealousy. Stella is the first of McGrath's significant female figures; her tragic story raises questions about gender because, in spite of her centrality in the novel, its narrative voice means that her consciousness remains inaccessible to the reader, and her thoughts and – sometimes – actions remain the subject of speculation.

Stella Raphael is throughout an enigmatic and ambiguous figure, both victim and monster. In some respects she may be seen as a mid twentieth-century Gothic heroine, whose flight from the oppressive Victorian values of her marriage and the asylum itself is brought full circle when she is brought back, not as the wife of the deputy super-intendent, but as Cleave's patient. Bored and unfulfilled as the wife of a sexually indifferent husband, Max, and mother of a ten-year-old son, Charlie, she embarks upon an affair with Edgar. When he escapes, she follows him to London, where she lives with him and his friend, Nick, in bohemian squalor. She becomes terrified by his obsessive jealousy and runs away, at first shielded by Nick (with whom she has a distasteful sexual encounter), but then picked up by the police, who are searching for Edgar, and returned to her husband, who has lost his job as a result of her behaviour. He insists that they try to resume their family life, taking a post as a staff psychologist in an asylum in north Wales. There follows a period of intense unhappiness for all three of them in their new rented rural home. Stella becomes increas-ingly depressed and alcoholic, and succumbs to joyless sex with their mean-spirited landlord. This miserable exile culminates in a shockingly tragic event: accompanying her son on a school trip, she sits by and does nothing as he drowns in a deep pool. As Cleave puts it, 'You had to explain it, a child was dead; either she was a monster or she was mad' (199). Because the latter explanation is accepted in court, Stella finds herself back in the hospital where it had all started, this time as a patient, whom Cleave has promised to treat and make well. She is an inmate in the asylum where she had once had status as wife of the deputy superintendent. When her mental state appears to have improved, Cleave suggests not only that she might be well enough to leave, but that she should leave as his wife. However, she commits suicide by taking an overdose before this happens.

McGrath had much to draw on for his representation of life in the asylum. He is happy to talk about his childhood experiences of growing up at Broadmoor. Indeed, he recognizes that he has spoken so much about his early life that it 'does seem to have taken on a life of its own', as he remarked to one interviewer.[43] He recognizes that his father's profession has had a profound effect on his writing:

> So my father as a youngish man was at the cutting edge of new thinking in psychiatry, and he brought that energy into making it his life's work to reform this place. And he talked about it with great passion to his children, and long before I could really understand what he was telling me, I was absorbing details of his work, but also

catching his fierceness and enthusiasm for this project. I think that made a deep, deep impression, because it was the first strong message of the world I was living in, what my dad was up to behind those high walls. And that was probably the best childhood that a novelist could hope to have, and when I did start to write, it shouldn't have surprised me that up bubbled this fascination with extreme mental disturbance.[44]

It appears that the McGrath household was accustomed to hearing about the gruesome details of some of the patients' crimes. Dr McGrath, while remaining discreet about individuals, relished the more outlandish of these.[45] The young Patrick was also used to mixing with the safer prisoners, such as 'my friend Dennis, who killed his mother and boiled her eyeballs'.[46] Such a background provided rich material for a novelist and, by his own account, the preoccupations of McGrath's fiction have been shaped by these early experiences.

This biographical influence needs to be considered alongside the cultural history of the asylum and its relationship with Gothic, however. Foucault's substantial chapter on 'The Birth of the Asylum' in *Madness and Civilization* offers a historical context for McGrath's childhood experiences, but also reminds us that the realm of the fantastic had been subjected to the 'great confinement' of the eighteenth century:

> What the classical period had confined was not only an abstract un-reason which mingled madmen and libertines, invalids and criminals, but also an enormous reservoir of the fantastic, a dormant world of monsters supposedly engulfed in the darkness of Hieronymus Bosch which had spewed them forth. One might say that the fortresses of confinement added to their social role of segregation and purification a quite opposite cultural function. Even as they separated reason from unreason on society's surface, they preserved in depth the images where they mingled and exchanged properties.[47]

Foucault's observation contextualizes Edgar Stark, whose artistic impulses and paranoid jealousy have combined to make him criminally insane. Foucault, in his account of the developments of the classical period, also historicizes the asylum's carefully sustained order, which in this novel provides the context for Stella's profound transgression of sexual involvement with a patient:

> Formerly the house of confinement had inherited, in the social sphere, the almost absolute limits of the lazar house; it was a foreign country. Now the asylum must represent the continuity of social morality. The values of family and work, all the acknowledged virtues, now reign in the asylum.[48]

McGrath sets his novel in 1959, just before the decade that was to see a radical departure from the legacy of Victorian sexual morality in Britain; 'sexual intercourse began in 1963', as the much-quoted line from a Larkin poem puts it.[49] The 1960s were also to see a change of attitude towards the confinement of the mentally ill, and subsequent decades saw widespread closure of large institutions and the discontinued use of the term 'asylum'. Cleave notes very early in the novel that 'the Mental Health Act had just been passed into law' (2). This Act abolished the distinction between psychiatric and other hospitals and encouraged the development of community care. The use of the term 'bins' by the psychiatrists in McGrath's novel (see, for example, p. 44) echoes a common colloquialism of this earlier period in the twentieth century, whereby asylums were referred to as 'loony bins'. Cleave reflects on the high-security asylum in which he has spent 'the best years' of his life. Built on 'the standard Victorian linear model', 'this is a moral architecture' which 'embodies regularity, discipline, and organization'. It is a 'grim carceral' architecture, the boundaries of which are shored up and secured (2). Thus, it provides a fitting backdrop to the beginning – and end – of Stella's story. Just as Edgar breaches the boundaries of the asylum, she breaches the boundaries of her marriage and the oppressive gender ideology that underpins it.

It is no coincidence that her husband is described as having 'an affection for all things Victorian' (3); ironically, this affection leads him to welcome the introduction of Edgar and his talents into his garden to restore the architecture of the conservatory. The image of the garden, as has already been noted, is recurrent in McGrath's fiction. In this novel, the garden of the Raphaels' house is the scene of Stella's 'fall'; an echo of the biblical Fall in which the primal female transgression, the sin of female sexuality, is enacted. Although Cleave admits, 'it has not been easy to talk to Stella about the sex' (22), she tells him that this is the place where it had first occurred between her and Edgar. More precisely, at his suggestion, she had 'pulled him into the conservatory' (23), the site of Max's desire for Victorian restoration. This garden has already partly reverted to nature through neglect: 'what had once been the front lawn . . . had become a meadow of thick grass and wild flowers' (22). There is a parallel here with Stella herself, who, in a conversation at a dinner party about psychiatrists' marriages, complains, 'Most of us are dying of chronic neglect' (45). Although she suspects that Max's ambition is 'to tame and cultivate both the hospital and the estate, make them over as his twin gardens' (26), he takes his wife's role for granted and is deeply shocked when it becomes apparent that she is neither tame nor cultivated. The path she takes, however, leads out of the garden; her last conversation with Cleave before she and Max leave for Wales is in the same garden, now autumnal and redolent of decay: 'She was paler, slower, heavier; there was a gravity about her now. The apple trees were heavily laden, and the ground beneath was scattered with fallen fruit, soft, spongy apples, pale green and yellow, dimpled with black spots of rot' (145). His words to her here intimate the proximity of passion and delirium when he says, 'I'm a doctor. I don't blame someone for becoming ill. So how could I blame you for falling in love' (145). This compassionate but also dispassionate discourse is contextualized by the description of the decaying autumnal garden, which suggests an analogy with Stella herself.

In a novel concerned with boundaries, Stella is multiply transgressive; in her relationship with Edgar, she had (in Cleave's words) 'eroticized the patient body' (27). In so doing, she had metaphorically breached the boundaries of the asylum as surely as Edgar had by entering her house, then her bedroom and finally breaking out of the asylum itself. Stella's story throws into relief the way in which social attitudes constrained women in the mid twentieth century. The boundaries of the asylum are paralleled by the ideological boundaries that contain her as a middle-class married woman and which she breaches, just as surely as Edgar breaches the physical boundaries of the asylum. The superintendent says to her (by way of a warning) of the paranoid patients, 'We can manage them, we can contain them, but we don't really know how to treat them. Because we don't really know what they are', and she wonders, 'Is he talking about his patients . . . or women?' (69). The structuring device of the annual dance provides another frame for the events of the novel, which cover one year, although it is clear that the story is being told some time after, as Cleave introduces his narrative with the words, 'Stella Raphael's story is one of the saddest I know' (1). Sander L. Gilman notes how dances became a regular feature of Victorian asylums.[50] The dance reflects a historical practice which, according to Gilman, demonstrates 'how narrow is the line between the sane and the mad; how close the external world is to the world of the asylum'. The reverse is true, he adds, in that it shows 'how close insanity can be brought to sanity through the liberating moment of carnival, a festivity felt to be within the bounds of Victorian propriety'.[51] In *Asylum*, the dance plays a pivotal role in the plot, its carnivalesque quality suggested by Cleave's comment that 'for this one evening they [parole patients from both male and female wings] and the staff become an extended family without distinction of rank and status' (4). The first dance is the occasion, we discover later, at which Edgar demonstrates his sexual desire for Stella; they are already acquainted through his work in the garden of her house on the hospital's estate.

The early account of the dance in the novel, however, places Stella as subject of the male gaze. Seen through Cleave's eyes, Stella is subjected to a detailed description covering the finer points of her dress ('a low-cut black evening dress of coarse ribbed silk, an exquisite grosgrain I had never seen before') and her physical qualities:

> I know she was considered beautiful: her eyes were much remarked on, and she had a pale, almost translucent complexion and thick blonde hair, almost white, cut rather short, that she brushed straight off her forehead. She was a rather fleshy, full-breasted woman, taller than the average, and that night she was wearing a single string of pearls that nicely set off the whiteness of her neck and shoulders and bosom. (5–6)

This and the prior observation about the dress suggest aesthetic appreciation. The opening phrase is telling: this is not an expression of sexual attraction, but instead a cool appraisal of a woman's attributes. Indeed, the sense of distancing here makes sense of a question Edgar asks of Cleave much later: 'What would she want with an old queen like you?' (236). Cleave's use of the word 'fleshy' is a portent of the events that are to follow, when Stella appears to have succumbed helplessly to the demands of the flesh.

Cleave paints Stella's marriage as arid; married young, she now feels neglected by her husband, whose sexual interest in her is tepid at best. She refers to herself as 'the invisible woman' (87). In contrast with the 'animal vitality' of Edgar (6), Max is 'a reserved, rather melancholy man'. 'It was obvious to me the first time I met them that he wasn't the type to satisfy a woman like Stella', comments Cleave (1). Stella's life as wife of the deputy superintendent is framed by Victorian attitudes: she is expected to behave as a dutiful wife and mother in a family which relies partly on the patronage of Max's imperious mother, Brenda, for its prosperity. Cleave relishes the formal structure of the hospital and the opportunities it affords him to treat the 'custodial staff' with 'a sort of patrician affability' (39), and comments to Brenda, in relation to Max's ambitions, that 'it is tempting ... to run one of these large, closed hospitals. To exercise Victorian paternalism on the grand scale' (44).

As well as breaking out of the sexual boundaries of such an arrangement, Stella also violates the expectations of motherhood. Her son Charlie is initially the link between her and Edgar, as, like the young Patrick, he makes friends with the patient working in the garden. Edgar takes advantage of this relationship by telling Stella that he has a son of the same age whom he has not seen for more than five years: 'All lies. Edgar has no son', Cleave tells the reader (12). The parental bond is drastically weakened by her passion for Edgar; 'that child has a malicious imagination', she says to Max when he admits that Charlie had told him she had come home drunk from London (89). In the same conversation she accuses 'that boy' of 'telling tales' on her (90). She leaves Charlie behind in her flight to London; when she is brought back and Max attempts to reconstitute the family in a new setting, her reluctance makes Charlie deeply unhappy, to the extent that she is challenged about his state of mind by his teacher. It is after she discovers that Edgar has made his way to nearby Chester and is in police custody that Charlie's tragic death takes place, as a result of what seems to be the extreme of dereliction of maternal duty: she stands by, smoking, while Charlie drowns. The scene is witnessed by the teacher, who blames her for Charlie's death. 'Why didn't you shout?' is Max's question, one that is echoed in the police station (199). Cleave has already offered an explanation to the reader: Edgar's arrest was the turning point for Stella: 'All lost. There could be no more fantasy of flight and escape. It all collapsed then the entire structure. And it's at this point I think we can say that Stella sinks into clinical depression' (192).

This is a key point in the pathologization of Stella; for Cleave the drowning is explicable in terms of psychiatric theory:

> The literature on maternal filicide is not large but it is clear: usually an extended suicide, the removal of a child from a situation which the mother finds intolerable, though in Stella's case complicated by the projection on to the child of the intense hostility she felt towards its father; a classic Medea complex. (208)

For much of the time, Cleave speaks in the language of the psychiatrist; there are moments, however, when a Gothic discourse irrupts into his narrative, as when he describes Stella wandering through London: ' A sad woman drifting down sad streets, insubstantial, not quite real, not quite there, a ghost' (140). In the hospital, Cleave tells her she must make peace with Max and, according to his version of their meeting, she wondered 'What did she look like to him? . . . The slut who'd ruined his life was now the pale fat witch who'd drowned his son' (201). The narrative leaves open the possibility that Stella has retained a grand passion for Edgar right up until her suicide. What prompts this act is open to interpretation, but her thwarted desire for Edgar, once she knows that he, too, is in the hospital and unattainable, remains a distinct possibility. When Cleave relates that he had suggested that their relationship had begun as 'just a case of household lust', he 'felt a flare of spirited hostility from her' (9). Early in the novel he had reflected that at the beginning of the affair, Stella had excused Edgar's crime as 'a simple crime of passion, which of course permitted her to romanticize him' (21). Cleave's final judgement on their relationship is made clear on the opening page of the novel:

she was a romantic. She translated her experience with Edgar Stark into the stuff of melodrama, she made of it a tale of outcast lovers braving the world's contempt for the sake of a great passion. Four lives were destroyed in the process, but whatever remorse she may have felt she clung to her illusions until the end. (1)

Edgar himself emerges from Cleave's account of him as a complex figure: a challenging case for treatment, 'my Edgar', as he refers to him (20). In Edgar, the obsessive passion of the artist transfers itself into obsessive possessiveness towards the women with whom he has relationships. Cleave admits that he had been 'intrigued' by Edgar from the start, describing him as 'a forceful individual with an original mind . . . possessed of considerable charm', but also as 'a devious intelligence, quick to grasp the workings of the hospital and always alert to its own interest' (3). He also claims an affinity between art and psychiatry: 'I have always been fascinated by the artistic personality, I think because the creative impulse is so vital a quality in psychiatry, certainly it is in my own clinical work' (3). Diagnosed as suffering from a paranoid psychosis, Edgar's crime and subsequent incarceration had been prompted by an obsessive jealousy of his wife and his suspicion (unfounded, according to Cleave) that she was serially unfaithful to him. Cleave rations for the reader his explication of the crime that had caused Edgar to be imprisoned, hinting at worse than murder: 'it was what he did to her *after* that that indicated to us how very disturbed he was' (8). The superintendent reveals to Stella, in medical terms, that Edgar had decapitated and enucleated his wife, Ruth, and then translates this into everyday language: 'He cut her head off and then he took her eyes out' (69). It is not until the end of the novel, however, that Cleave reveals to the reader that after cutting off his wife's head, Edgar had 'stuck it on his sculpture stand. Then he'd worked it with his tools as though it were a lump of damp clay' (237).

This act of perverted artistic possession could well have been Stella's fate, Cleave believes. He relates Edgar's 'morbid jealousy' (42) to his artistic temperament. Cleave, the connoisseur of paintings, has a jaundiced view of artists, seeing Edgar's 'deep and childish need to elevate, and idealize, the love object' as 'not uncommon in artists', adding:

The very nature of their work, the long periods of isolation, followed
by public self-display, and the associated risk of rejection, all conspire
to create unnaturally intense relationships with their sexual partners.
Then when the disillusion occurs, as of course it must, the sense of
betrayal is profound, and will in some individuals translate into a
pathological conviction of the other's duplicity. (43)

It is in the final phase of the novel that the affinity between Edgar
and Cleave becomes apparent. Indeed, the significance of Cleave's
name, with its connotations of splitting as well as clinging, is thrown
into relief as the doubling so common in Gothic fiction is made
clear. Edgar is Mr Hyde to Cleave's Dr Jekyll. Both are driven by the
impulse towards possession: with Edgar this leads to the atrocities
perpetrated on the body of another; in the case of Cleave the desire
for possession takes a different form, but the implication is that
psychiatry itself holds the potential to be a Gothic undertaking.
During Stella's own incarceration, discussions in therapy with Cleave
give him some of the detail of her story. This is the culmination of
his surveillance, not just of Edgar, but of Stella herself (he tells the
reader early in the novel that one of the custodial staff reported to
him the 'budding friendship' (29) between the two). Although he
does not refer to Stella as 'my Stella' until after she is dead, his
actions indicate a different kind of possession, so that eventually he
offers her marriage (after a divorce from Max) as a different kind of
asylum: safety. At this moment in the narrative there seems to be
direct access to Stella's consciousness: 'She felt like a consignment of
damaged but retrievable womanhood, in the process of being trans-
ferred from old owner to new, after being stored for a while in a
warehouse' (228). It is difficult to tell whether this is Stella herself or
Cleave's assumption. He has already told the reader that he has 'more
than once imagined her in my house . . . among my furniture, my
books, my art. Oh, she had a place there, among my fine objects' (219).
   Much of the narrative has been about Stella's body, but the twin
figures of Edgar and Cleave are both fixated on her head. In Edgar's
case, the physical head itself is an obsession; his first request to Stella
in the garden is that he be allowed to sketch her head. For Cleave,
it is the metaphorical head. In his role as psychiatrist, with motives
he believes to be benign, he seeks to shape and control what is

going on inside her head – to the point where he can add her to 'the fine objects' in his handsome house. Ultimately he does, but it is Stella's head as sculpted by Edgar, whittled down to: 'a thin, beautiful, tiny, anguished head now, no bigger than my hand; but it is her. I often take it out, over the course of the day, and admire it. So, you see, I do have my Stella after all' (250). This expression of satisfaction carries resonances of Browning's poem, 'My Last Duchess', in which a murderous Duke cherishes the image of his dead wife, having done away with the living original. Cleave's last statement provides a chilling end to the novel: 'And, of course, I still have him' (250).

The film of *Asylum* is the least successful of the three adaptations to date. Whereas McGrath himself scripted the other two, this one has a screenplay by Patrick Marber. The film charts in a linear fashion the events that lead to the death of Stella's son and her return to the asylum as a patient. It is very late in acknowledging the involvement of Cleave, adopting an intermittent voice-over in the seductive tones of Ian McKellen, who plays him. For much of the time, this is a drab and depressing tale of self-destruction presented in filmic realism. It does, however, give Stella a more Gothic death scene than the novel allows: she flings herself from a high tower in the asylum, creating a visually melodramatic climax to the narrative. Not surprisingly, the critics were cruel, finding rich ground for mockery in the melodrama: 'Bored Wife and Mad Hunk, Alone Together' and 'Shrink's wife flops on her back for wife-killer inmate in his "Asylum", but fails to earn an understanding of why', are just two examples.[52] Thus, the film fails to do justice to the subtlety with which McGrath transmutes the Gothic's traditional concerns with anxiety about identity, transgression and decay into a powerful exploration of the destructive potential of both art and psychiatry.

These three novels of the 1990s – *Spider, Dr Haggard's Disease* and *Asylum* – offer a striking fictional representation of madness, in stories rooted in their time and place. In *Asylum* madness, obsession and art are closely linked; these are concerns that also inform the fiction that follows in the next decade. In the switch of setting away from mid twentieth-century England, however, other concerns also begin to emerge more strongly, as the unreliability of narration becomes more emphatically not only personal, but also cultural and political.

3

Worlds New and Old

༮༼

The later period of McGrath's fiction reflects the move from England to North America he had made earlier in his life, going to work in Canada and never returning to live permanently in Britain. Although he now spends some time in England, his main home is in New York. The preoccupations of the earlier fiction are still discernible in these later works but they are inflected in different ways. The later fiction is concerned more overtly with 'history' as well as individual histories. Medicine and the diseases of the mind remain ever present, however, and the vexed figure of the artist takes centre stage in *Port Mungo*. After Stella Raphael comes a series of interesting female characters, beginning with the memorable and eponymous Martha Peake. All of the later work is haunted in some way by the Gothic, in spite of McGrath's insistence that he does not want to be regarded as a Gothic novelist. The millennial novel *Martha Peake* (the very name of which combines both stereotypical homeliness and the parodic Gothic prose of Mervyn Peake) makes this haunting thematic in its treatment of the Old World and the New in the late eighteenth century, a point in history that witnessed not only the American Revolution but also the emergence of Gothic fiction in England.

Martha Peake (2000)

Like the earlier novels, *Martha Peake* presents a challenge to the reader. Apparently a historical novel, its self-reflexive narrative positions it not only in relation to historical events but also in relation to different fictional conventions, of which the Gothic is the most dominant. In parodying what is already recognized as a liminal mode of writing (in which boundaries and their transgression are the most persistent features), it creates new liminal spaces in the reading process itself. Like all parody, it relies upon the reader's ability to recognize 'repetition with critical difference'.[1] Not only does Gothic articulate the transgression of boundaries, but as a mode of writing it constantly threatens to transgress its own boundaries. Realism itself, it would seem, is haunted by Gothic, a haunting that creates particularly disturbing effects in the liminal space between the two discourses; texts haunted in this way might be termed 'liminal Gothic'. In *Martha Peake*, the last of McGrath's playful post-modern novels, this is foregrounded in a self-reflexive manner. Written in a cultural context where it must relate to the already written, using and subverting discourses that are already familiar to the reader, it 'plays seriously with the structures of authority. It exists in the liminal space between power and subversion', to quote Alison Lee's description of postmodern fiction.[2]

In *Martha Peake*, McGrath was to return to his initial impulse of playing with the well-established conventions of Gothic. For those expecting a more conventional historical novel (it is subtitled 'a novel of the revolution'), there was to be disappointment in store. Un-favourable descriptions on the Amazon review site include 'derivative, turgid crap', 'the most depressing, appalling, horrible book I have ever read' and 'this mess' from another reader, who then elaborates:

> By the end I was so tuned out I may have just missed it, but I never quite figured out what the point was of having one man narate [sic] a story to another who then proceeded to make up his own third version of the same story. He really had no knowledge of the situation except what the second man told him and yet he decided most of what he was told must be wrong and proceeded to make up his own third version completely counter to the version he was being told.

Most reviewers confessed to being disappointed that what claimed to be 'a novel of the revolution' was not a 'reliable' historical novel at all.[3]

Martha Peake, therefore, appears to have confounded the expectations of 'everyreader', who, not unreasonably, seems to have expected a more conventional story, one which might have presented a linear, apparently authoritative narrative. Such a narrative might have exhibited Lukács's defining characteristic of the historical novel, presenting a microcosm which generalizes.[4] In Barthes's terms, McGrath's 'writerly' text disappointed those who had wanted something more 'readerly'. *Martha Peake* is a self-conscious exercise in exploring the liminal spaces between Gothic convention and reader expectations; it is precisely those qualities that seem to disappoint that are of interest in this densely and mischievously intertextual novel. Set in the late eighteenth century, the period of the early Gothic novel, it plays different novelistic discourses off against each other in an exploration of revolutionary myth-making and the genesis of 'the American Dream'. What are now seen as clichés of Gothic fiction are deployed as part of a complex and unreliable narration; in the 'English' parts of the novel, McGrath has his narrator place himself in such a Gothic novel. Here the Gothic affect (defined by Chris Baldick as combining 'a fearful sense of inheritance in time with a claustrophobic sense of enclosure in space') is represented, rather than created in the reader, through excessive, parodic effect.[5]

Attempting to outline the plot of such a novel is a dangerous undertaking; the very attempt highlights the unreliability of the storytelling. *Martha Peake* is not lacking in story, however. Some time in the 1820s, a man of imaginative inclination, Ambrose Tree, rides out to visit his ancient and ageing Uncle William, who lives still in the mouldering Drogo Hall on Lambeth Marsh which had been left to him many years before by the anatomist Lord Drogo, to whom he was a loyal assistant. The childless William Tree has summoned his nephew, who is his heir, so that he may tell him the tale of Harry Peake and his daughter Martha. In those days, Lambeth Marsh was not some remote location but hard on the centre of the Old World itself, lying in a bend of the Thames south-west of the City of London. The building in 1750 of Westminster Bridge (eulogized by Wordsworth in his famous poem of 1802 and alluded to in the novel) had opened up this area to the trade and travel of London itself. During Martha's time in London, some fifty years earlier, it would have been a border-land, itself a liminal space, within sight of the encroaching city. At the time of Ambrose's visit to William, London (which he describes as a 'great toad smoking and stinking in the distance') would already have been reaching out into the marsh; in Ambrose's dotage, the London slums – sites of a later Victorian Gothic – would have colonized much of it.[6] William's purpose in insisting that his nephew hear Martha's story is withheld until the end of the novel – and much of what we read is supplied by Ambrose himself. 'Much of the detail I have had to supply from my own imagination, that is from the ardent sympathetic understanding of the tragic events my uncle William described', he tells us (6).

This is the tale he tells: Harry is a Cornishman, but after losing his wife and breaking his back in a fire associated with his illegal 'free trade' activities, he travels, a giant of a man but now hunchbacked, to London with his eight-year-old daughter, Martha. There he makes a living as a performing poet, his appeal much enhanced by the freakery of his monstrous appearance, while Martha 'ripens' into an early adulthood. He dreams of a new world through his radical epic 'The Ballad of Joseph Tresilion', the popularity of which leads to his being dubbed 'Harry America'. Gin, pain and despair do their worst with Harry, however, making him mad and leading him ultimately to behave monstrously, raping his devoted daughter. Fearing for her safety, Martha seeks sanctuary in Drogo Hall but her love for her father means that she continues to meet him out on the marsh. Her vio-lation (which, she is convinced, has made her pregnant) finally makes Martha decide to accept William's offer of a passage to New England. It is the autumn of 1774.

At this point, on the basis of the crumbling fragments of paper that are the remains of Martha's letters (a 'found' document of Gothic convention) and his own vivid imagination, Ambrose creates a narra-tive of Martha's experiences in America. Although suffering from marsh fever, he tells this with the clarity of a romantic realism. Martha is taken in by the family of her aunt, who is the wife of a rich merchant, Silas Rind, in the fishing port of New Morrock. She marries Silas's son, Adam, and gives birth to Harry's son, who bears his misshapen back. Although a fervent believer in the revolutionary cause, she betrays the community – in exchange for the promise of news of her father – to the naval officer who had interrogated her when she disembarked at Boston. Convinced that Harry Peake had been lured into Drogo Hall so that his skeleton could be exhibited in 'the Museum of Anatomy', Ambrose conjectures that the officer, resonantly named Giles Hawkins,[7] tells her that Harry is dead.

Martha's tragic story is continued by William. When the English navy later bombards New Morrock, killing those unable to flee, he relates, Martha returns to the wharf with a musket and shoots the officer, wounding him. She is killed instantly by a returning volley; in the telling of this, William is overcome by emotion. Although Silas Rind appears to know of her role in the bombardment, he is instrumental in promoting the legend of her defiance of the British, because 'the Revolution required a martyr'. It does not matter, he tells his daughter, 'that the legend is a lie' (317). This late phase of the narrative is punctuated by Ambrose's account of his venture into the bowels of Drogo Hall, which he now believes to be haunted. Dissuaded of this possibility, he then speculates that Lord Drogo, whom he believes to be evil, is still alive and chasing after him. This belief leads him to shoot at an intruder in his room, apparently killing him. The intruder turns out to be none other than Harry Peake, who has lived there for the previous fifty years after being nursed back to health by Lord Drogo who, far from being evil, is now shown to be a benevolent physician. He has not in fact been shot but is so deeply shocked by the experience of the near miss that he fails fast and dies within a few days. William dies soon afterwards and Ambrose inherits Drogo Hall. He concludes his tale, himself now the Hall's ancient master, by telling the reader that 'all this was written long ago' (339).

In *Martha Peake*, McGrath is engaging with the historical specificity of early definitions of Gothic as a genre located at the end of the eighteenth century. The novel invites the reader into a playful engagement with a variety of novelistic discourses. It opens with the words of its primary narrator, Ambrose Tree, with an implicit caveat for the reader of historical fiction: 'It is a black art, the writing of history, is it not – to resurrect the dead and animate their bones, as historians do?' (3); this novel, it suggests, will be 'historiographical metafiction' (to use Linda Hutcheon's coinage) with a distinctly Gothic emphasis, its narrative project likened to Dr Frankenstein's creation of his monster. The interrogative insists immediately on the complicity of the reader, the reader who is prepared to continue with a narrative in this vein. Of course, McGrath is by no means an innovator in creating fiction from what we now perceive as the problematics of historical narrative. Such exponents as John Fowles (most notably in *The French Lieutenant's Woman*), Graham Swift, Peter Carey and Peter Ackroyd had already developed the mode. Linda Hutcheon's 1988 book, *A Poetics of Postmodernism*, articulates the postmodern dilemmas of both history and fiction:

> In both fiction and history writing today, our confidence in empiricist and positivist epistemologies has been shaken – shaken, but perhaps not yet destroyed. And this is what accounts for the scepticism rather than any real denunciation; it also accounts for the defining paradoxes of postmodern discourses . . . Historiographical metafiction, for example, keeps distinct its formal auto-representation and its historical context, and in so doing problematizes the very possibility of historical knowledge, because there is no reconciliation, no dialectic here – just unresolved contradiction.[8]

For the aged and ailing Ambrose, the difficulties presented by the very possibility of historical knowledge are a source of anguish rather than intellectual play:

> as I look back over the pages I wrote during those fraught days which culminated in Harry Peake's death I wonder that I am still sane. For at times, now, I glimpse a past that is no more than a catalogue of sacrifice and abomination and heroism and resolve and victory, and sunk in shadow are the lies and muddles and myriad random workings of chance in the thing, and to bring it all together in one coherent whole – why, the human mind is not up to it! And I am convinced that history can unhinge the brain, that a man might be *driven mad* by history – ! (339)

Ambrose's desire for coherence is undercut for the reader by the way in which the novel represents his discourse. One of McGrath's characteristically unreliable narrators, his reconstruction of Martha's story is, often anachronistically, shaped by fictional resonances that the novel's twenty-first century readers will recognize. His, and the novel's, closing words, for example, are evocative of *Wuthering Heights's* Cathy and Heathcliff:

> And if Harry's spirit still wanders the Lambeth Marsh, as I believe it does, for I hear him at times when the wind is up, and the rain hammers at the windows, and the wild dogs howl – then I know that Martha rises from the Old Burying Ground and ascends the great headland of the cape, whence her spirit flies out to him across the North Atlantic, and they are, at last, and for ever, as one – ha! (340)

That is the final word of the novel – 'ha!' (with exclamation mark). What can the reader make of this? That Ambrose's overheated imagination cannot be trusted? Or that he is expressing glee at a narrative brought to a satisfactory conclusion, the black art of the animator of history's bones, pleased with his own cleverness?

These are questions to keep in mind when considering the framing narrative of Martha's tale. A simplistic reading of the novel might tempt one to see old decadent England represented as Gothic in contrast to the Romantic freedoms demanded by the New World. This is Ambrose's construct, however, and it is his narrative that renders the representation of England Gothic. For the reader, there is ample evidence that this is a parodic Gothic: Ambrose *Gothicizes* his experiences at Drogo Hall. It is an overblown narrative, full of clichés, instantly recognizable to anyone familiar with the Gothic fiction of the last two hundred or so years. On the very first page, he evokes the 'drear landscape' of the place, his journey to it undertaken alone, carrying a loaded pistol; he is met by an aged servant who then disappears, leaving him alone with William, whom he describes as not being 'long for this world', with his skin 'white and brittle as paper' (4). Drogo Hall itself is equipped by Ambrose's narrative with the full architecture of the Gothic, such features noted by Eve Kosofsky Sedgwick in her work on Gothic conventions.[9] An Early Georgian house, it is abutted by the original hall and older buildings which, Ambrose tells the reader, 'were built in a manner suggestive not of the Age of Reason but of an earlier age, a Dark Age' (90). He writes of his first morning there: 'Ghosts and secrets: I encountered locked corridors, sealed rooms, doors that opened on to walls. But I did not encounter Percy or any other living soul, although I was aware at times of low voices in nearby passages' (23).

Ambrose's perception of Drogo Hall as a Gothic edifice colours his perception of its long-dead owner, Lord Francis Drogo. In the figure of Francis, Gothic's ambivalent relationship with science is fore-grounded. From *Frankenstein*, through *The Island of Dr Moreau* and into the twentieth and twenty-first centuries, the Gothic scientist is one who employs rationality to effect abomination. Ambrose's scientist is a dealer in death, abetted by his own 'resurrection man', Clyte, who brings him fresh bodies from the gallows – and goodness knows where else, it is hinted. The Clyte of Ambrose's account is an abject figure, described at one point as 'spidery' (55). The secrets and ghosts that Ambrose believes he senses in Drogo Hall are connected with the monstrosity he has made of Lord Drogo in his mind. His journey into the penetralium of the house, the Museum of Anatomy, 'through the chill malodorous passages that riddled the vaults and cellars' of what he calls 'this malignant dying house' (287) is told with appropriate Gothic suspense and relish, bringing together not only some of the Gothic conventions of Ambrose's time but a strong whiff of Poe's in-carcerating spaces, along with, in the rotting specimens, the oleaginous slime of the 'abhuman', as identified by the work of Kelly Hurley and others in late Victorian Gothic. Failing to find the shocking secret he believes is there, Harry Peake's skeleton, Ambrose's account adds terror to horror, as he concludes with the page-turning line: 'And then, in the silence, with a last flare in the shivering gloom, one wall sconce in the ante-chamber gave out with a sputtering sigh – and then, a second later, the other – and in the sudden darkness, *a hand fell on my shoulder*' (289). Later, waking in his bed and unable to offer any other rational conclusion, he conjectures (with shades of Poe and Conan Doyle and evoking the monkeys of McGrath's short stories) that it must have been 'some creature, a small ape, perhaps, which years ago had escaped from Drogo's menagerie and lived like a troglo-dyte in those labyrinthine cellars' (305). Such is the accumulation of Gothic cliché that the narrative transcends any charge of derivative-ness or plagiarism. This is almost a celebration of Gothic itself, much in the way that Umberto Eco sees the cult film *Casablanca* as trans-formative of cinematic cliché: 'When all the archetypes burst out shamelessly, we plumb Homeric profundity. Two clichés make us laugh but a hundred clichés move us because we sense dimly that the clichés are talking among themselves, celebrating a reunion.'[10]

The Gothicization of place that Ambrose's narrative asserts is key to his Gothic narrative of the Old World as diseased, corrupt and decayed. It is, however, undermined by the very specific location chosen by McGrath; this Gothicization of place for McGrath's text also offers contrary signs to the alert reader, undermining the parodic Gothic and hinting at another kind of discourse, and creating liminal moments in Ambrose's narrative. An unusual name, 'Drogo', as well as suggesting the evil Count Dracula, evokes the twelfth-century Saint Drogo who was venerated for his compassion, humility and kindness to people suffering from mental illness and who was also himself beset by an unsightly bodily affliction.[11] Significant, too, is McGrath's choice of Lambeth Marsh as the setting for Drogo Hall, the place of enunciation for the tale of Martha. Its name, deriving from the Anglo-Saxon 'Lambhythe' (meaning 'loamy' or muddy landing-place), suggests a long history. Francis Moore, astrologer and physician and originator of *Old Moore's Almanac*, lived there in the sixteenth century. As Peter Ackroyd points out in his 'biography of London': 'By chance or coincidence, many astrologers came to inhabit Lambeth. The name itself may have drawn them. Beth-el was in Hebrew the name for a sacred place, here fortuitously connected with the Lamb of God.'[12] William Blake lived in Lambeth between 1793 and 1800 and here wrote his visionary works, such as *Jerusalem*. Lambeth thus has old associations with the quest for enlightenment; the origins of modern science have roots here through the astrologers and alchemists. John Tradescant, the seventeenth-century horticultural explorer who appears in Jeanette Winterson's 1988 work of historiographical metafiction, *Sexing the Cherry*, lived in Lambeth and established a collection of objects of curiosity from his travels, which later became a museum. And, in 1815, the new Bethlem hospital for the insane, intended to be modern and enlightened, was built at Lambeth.

It is in the context of the parodic Gothic of Ambrose's framing narrative that his construction of Harry and Martha Peake as symbols of the American revolutionary spirit needs to be read. As he tells the reader by way of apology for his conjectures about facts: 'I have imagination. I have poetic intuition. I have the weight of symbolic necessity bearing down upon me' (333). Critics such as Jerrold E. Hogle and Robert Miles have argued for the role of Gothic as representing that which is abjected in the making of national identity.[13] Robert Mighall argues for Gothic embodying an attitude to the past: 'Epochs, institutions, places and people are Gothicized, have the Gothic thrust upon them. That which is Gothicized depends on history and the stories it needs to tell itself.'[14] What is Gothicized, he claims, 'depends on how each culture chooses to represent itself, and where it locates progress and its necessary antithesis'.[15] Yet such a process is not straightforward. As Ian Duncan points out, in the late eighteenth century:

> An unofficial, oppositional movement, populist and proto-nationalist in its appeal and with its ideological roots in the radical Whiggery [i.e. progressive politics] of the last century, was reclaiming 'Gothic' culture as the ancient constitutional source of British liberties usurped by the Norman Conquest and subsequent aristocratic rule . . . At the same time, the establishment concept of 'Gothic' was that of barbarian forces that had overthrown a civilization, and the long cultural darkness haunted by despotism and anarchy, superstition and enthusiasm, out of which the present British dispensation, modelling itself on classical principles, had only lately emerged.[16]

Ambrose's telling of Martha's story represents the Gothicization of the Old World in the making of a new national myth, one that he is impelled to believe in, possibly because of the aridity of his own life. In this context, Ambrose's Gothicization of his own culture through an unconsciously parodic Gothic narrative indicates the sceptical stance of the late twentieth century towards the processes of revolutionary myth-making, cultural abjection and attitudes towards the past; for Gothic discourses leach into his narrative of the New World, too, creating liminal moments and spaces in it. In his telling of Martha's part in the American War of Independence he appears to eschew his own Gothic sensibility in favour of a different set of conventions which themselves verge on cliché. Even in William's account of Harry's origins, McGrath hooks the reader through evoking some of the popular romantic literature of the nineteenth and twentieth centuries: Harry's Cornwall is a site of defiance and sublimity as celebrated through fiction – a literary West Country, the country of Daphne du Maurier, overlaid with Robert Louis Stevenson and J. Meade Falkner with its 'free trade' (smuggling). Even the name of Harry's dead wife, 'Grace Foy', has a self-conscious fictionality about it ('Foy' was the name that Sir Arthur Quiller-Couch gave to his daughter). Moreover, the representation of New England with its clean forests, bracing elements and wholesome kitchens is resonant of such American texts as Nathaniel Hawthorne's *The Blithedale Romance*, themselves subject to the liminal effects of Gothic haunting. Martha's home in New Morrock is, not accidentally, in the house of her Uncle Silas, evoking the Victorian Gothic novel of the same name by Sheridan LeFanu.

Harry Peake is framed in an open, sublime American landscape in his portrait in Drogo Hall (a parody of the ancestral portraits of Gothic texts). This is encountered by Ambrose on the second page of the novel:

> He stood against a wild moorland scene, a pine flattening in the gale on the brow of a distant hill, and rags of black cloud flying across the sky. [. . .] It was not a handsome face [. . .] but it was a strong, complicated face, hatched and knotted with sorrow and passion, a big stubborn chin uplifted – the whole head uplifted – lips unsmiling and slightly parted, and the expression one of defiance, yes, and purpose. (4)

It is much later in the novel, with much of Martha's story told, that he realizes that the man in the portrait has a straight back and, looking closer, reads the 'faded copperplate' of the nameplate on the frame: 'The American Within'. Harry's spine is freighted with significance for Ambrose. It is at once a Gothic signifier, an outward marker of the monstrosity that leads to the rape of his own daughter, the anatomical distinction that makes him prey to the evil Lord Drogo and the marker of America itself: 'And his broad back with its ridge of peaks down the spine – was it not the very image, in miniature, of the land itself? Was he not himself a *living map* of America?' (217). But in Ambrose's account, much is made of the straightness of the back of the symbolically named Adam, the young American man Martha marries and who accepts her hunchbacked baby as his own in the full knowledge that it is not. Ambrose imagines that Martha gives birth to a baby with Harry's spine, although the reader knows that this is biologically implausible, thus making the ambiguous sign of monstrosity become the distinguishing feature of America's future. Here is the liminality of Gothic at work: there is no clear boundary between what may pass in the realist novel and what is fantasy. Ambrose's Gothic discourse permeates the borders of his American vision, portending a future haunting; he appears powerless to resist its incursions.

In this is a novel that self-consciously revisits story-telling and the making of both novels and history; historical figures such as Tom Paine and heroines of the American Revolution, Molly Pitcher and Deborah Samson, make an appearance, but the reader is never allowed to forget the fictive nature of the history s/he is reading. The Gothicization of the Old World is undermined in the final ironic revelation that Harry Peake had lived to a ripe old age after having been cured of his madness by Lord Drogo, who

> had recently started upon a course of study in the diseases of the mind, realising as no other anatomist of his day would do, that the mental faculty was in principle no different from the other faculties of the human integral, and no less subject to disorder. (330–1)

Lambeth Marsh, in this final narrative turn, has become the location of reason and science. As Ambrose exclaims, 'large structures were collapsing in my mind' (325). Like all postmodern novels, this is as much a novel about writing as anything else. There are clues to Ambrose's own compulsion to reconstruct the narrative of American defiance through Martha and Harry Peake:

> I sat at my table with pen poised and dripping and thought of the portrait of Harry Peake hanging in my uncle's study. I am my mother's son and I too have an American within, but oh, he is trapped, as Harry's American was trapped; and like Harry's American he can only be conjured to life in art, which of course is no life at all! (279)

Yet Ambrose's very name, evocative of the cynical view of American life and liberty in the shape of Ambrose Bierce, suggests an ironic dual perspective at work in the novel. Such a construction of American defiance and its own belief in manifest destiny, it seems to suggest, is a romantic dream.

In an interview with Gilles Menegaldo in 1997, McGrath spoke of his plans for his new novel, suggesting that the writer of historical fiction may be compared with one of the most famous figures of Gothic fiction:

> I think one of the interesting ways one can think about the Frankenstein myth is to associate it with the process of composition, of invention, and for any writer attempting a historical novel, there are so many precedents that clearly you are always going to be putting together bits and pieces from previous writers, from histories and biographies; you are going to be cobbling together, patching together some sort of hybrid creature with leftovers from other texts.[17]

He also makes claims for the contemporary relevance of *Martha Peake*, which was published in the year that George W. Bush was first elected president. In an interview given in 2001, McGrath explained how the novel might be read in relation to contemporary America:

> The novel is a pastiche of the Gothic novels of the 18th century. My subject was America and I wanted to deal with America when it was a Romantic youth and not a crippled giant as it is today. I chose the American Revolution as part of the set for *Martha Peake* as I wanted to write about America, I wanted to understand how it is possible to love America when it is such a crippled ugly giant.[18]

If the 1991 collection *The New Gothic* was a significant landmark in the persistence of Gothic as a protean form, in *Martha Peake* there is something rather different at work: a self-reflexive engagement with Gothic narrative that foregrounds the liminality of the reading process it invites.

Port Mungo (2004)

In *Port Mungo*, McGrath returns to the twentieth century. Its protagonists, painter Jack Rathbone, his sister Gin (who narrates his story) and his lover, the artist Vera Savage, are all British – although not all English (Vera is a Glaswegian Scot). Most of the novel, however, is set in two locations, each Gothic in its own way: New York and Port Mungo itself, 'a once-prosperous river town now gone to seed, wilting and steaming among the mangrove swamps of the Gulf of Honduras',[19] described by one reviewer as 'the sort of setting that even Graham Greene might have found too seedy for fiction'.[20] According to McGrath, it is based on a place he had visited in Central America:

> When I went down to Belize, for instance, and saw what Belize City looks like – the shacks lurching unsteadily over the river, the mangrove swamps and so forth – that just told me, instantly, that here I had the setting of a novel. I took a lot of photos and then basically used what I'd seen.[21]

Although significant periods of Jack and Gin's life are spent in New York, it is Port Mungo that receives the most vivid and material representation in Gin's narrative, even though she herself spends only ten days there. Her account leaves the reader in no doubt of its primitive rawness and incipient violence, while at the same time invoking a series of stereotypes of sub-tropical squalor:

> On the waterfront I saw rough bars built of concrete blocks run by hard-faced Chinese and patronized by prostitutes and mean-looking men from off the boats. I remember dusty streets and alleyways, and canals, which stank, being open sewers, and disgorged into the river … I retain a vivid memory of the open market, where I saw a man split a live iguana down the belly with a machete, that reptile's flesh being a local delicacy. There were flies everywhere, noise, blood, the stench of butchered meat mingling with the fragrance of papaya and mango. (57)

It is an abject place; in contrast, New York is represented as a location of liminality, a spectral place where the past haunts the present and the self becomes unstable: 'people say that Manhattan breaks down the separation of inside and outside', says Gin (8). In contrast with the lushly painted landscapes of Port Mungo, the New York scenes of the novel are set in a series of interiors: Jack's loft; Gin's brownstone town-house and its attic, where Jack paints.

The novel tells the life story of Jack as told by his sister, Gin, who reveals herself early on to be an anything but impartial narrator. It is also the narrative of a woman whose life is dominated by one thing, her passionate love and admiration for her brother, which endures even as perspectives on the unfolding events prove to be relative. Jack and Gin are a pair of motherless siblings, close in age, who are both at art school in London. Already portrayed as a wild and sexually precocious child, Jack is besotted by a visiting Scottish artist, Vera Savage, and runs away with her to New York. He is seventeen. Desiring soon after to escape the sophisticated and clique-ridden New York art scene as well as the confines of the city, he takes off with Vera. They eventually arrive in Port Mungo, where they encounter an expatriate doctor, Johnny Hague, who (small world that it is) had been at medical school with Jack's older brother. Here the two artists wrestle with work and continue a suitably stormy and passionate relationship, or so we learn through Gin's conjectures (which are heavily coloured by accounts from her brother). Vera has an affair with the doctor. Two daughters, twelve years apart in age, are born and Vera leaves them for much of the time in the casual care of their father while she roams around the tropical landscape. The older, Peg, who has grown up wild and tough, is tragically drowned, aged sixteen, in the mangrove swamp. Jack's account of this tragedy (which echoes the death of young Charlie Raphael in *Asylum*) un-equivocally blames Vera. Shortly afterwards, Vera and Johnny arrange for the younger, Anna, to be sent to England to be brought up by her uncle; Jack does not oppose this course of action.

Grief-stricken, he returns to New York, but after a period of time pursuing a solitary existence in a loft and achieving a passing repu-tation with his primitivist style of painting (which he calls 'tropical-ism'), he is taken in by Gin and given a studio in her house. Their quiet existence is interrupted one day by the arrival of Anna, now grown up, who bears an uncanny resemblance to her dead sister and who, it transpires, has ambitions to be an artist herself. Jack becomes obsessed by her and Gin comes to suspect a different truth about the relationship between Peg and her father. This family secret of incest, this staple of the Gothic plot, emerges when Anna claims that Jack has made a sexual advance towards her and then, shortly after, he is found dead, having apparently committed suicide. This appears to vindicate Vera's account of Jack's destructive relationship with Peg, which, she claims, drove her daughter to suicide. Gin also becomes convinced by Vera's view that Jack's talent is very limited and recognizes its narcissism: 'He paints himself over and over again, I thought, it's all he ever does. Even his jungles are self-portraits, he told me so himself' (203). By the end of the novel, however, she has tipped back into denial and in a frenzied monologue convinces herself that Anna is responsible for Jack's death; this puts into perspective the assertion she makes at the opening of her narration: 'This was not a man who ever lost his moral compass, as Vera seems to believe – and certainly not a man who would take his own life! It's unthinkable. It makes a mockery of everything' (6–7).

Through a play of images, phrases and other cultural resonances, the novel brings together a set of accumulated conventions from Gothic literature and a set of cultural stereotypes concerning the artist in modernism in order to produce a distinctive postmodern critique of the modernist quest for artistic authenticity. In McGrath's earlier fiction, the artist is always represented as a pathological figure; in *Asylum* he is officially 'mad'. It is possible to read in the story of Jack Rathbone an exploration of the anxieties associated with the endeavours of the artist, be s/he painter or writer. The acknowledgements at the end of the novel, while expressing gratitude for the network of support the author has received, gesture clearly to the loneliness of the pursuit of writing and the anxieties attendant upon it: 'we go into the room alone, and we stay in the room alone'. This, however, may be a clichéd reading of a novel that works with clichés but never succumbs to them. In using the already written, *Port Mungo* hovers self-consciously on the edge of parody in new and disturbing ways; as the earlier chapters show, this is not a new practice for McGrath. Although *Port Mungo* is not a *roman-à-clef*, there are echoes of the lives of famous modernist artists. The post-Impressionist Gauguin is probably the most obvious, a figure who has come to epitomize the shedding of bourgeois convention through his embracing of personal and artistic freedom in a 'primitive' setting (in his case the South Seas). Gin describes Jack as 'this fiercely driven artist, this latter-day Gauguin' (80). His invention of the 'tropicalist' mode of painting seems to be a clear echo of Gauguin's work. Rothko is here, too, his suicide echoed in the manner of Jack's eventual self-destruction, slitting the arteries in his elbows rather than his wrists in his New York studio. Both of these historical figures are mentioned in the novel, thus forestalling any notion of fictionalized biography.

Gin's worship of her brother emphasizes Jack's masculinity. One incident from their adolescence which Gin believes 'must be included' in her account of their early years is the occasion when she surprises Jack with the governess, the wonderfully named Miss Helen Splendour. Whatever extra-curricular activity she had been providing involved Jack's 'penis up out of his trousers, emphatically erect' (20). Jack's tendency to flaunt the distinguishing mark of his sex is here rendered comically, but is represented in more sinister terms later in the novel. It seems likely that his death is triggered by his daughter's response to his exposure while she poses naked for him: 'He had it out', she says; all she saw was 'a contemptible, pathetic, dirty old man' (238). Jack as male and Jack as artist are bound together for Gin. His yearning for success is reflected in his leaving England for America and in his first view of New York:

> he experienced an intense excitement, so intense that it aroused him sexually, and with it as powerful an intimation as he'd ever felt that *greatness* lay within his grasp; and he could see no earthly reason why, with Vera beside him, he should not achieve all he knew he had it in him to achieve. (36–7)

Describing the personal and artistic crisis that led him to leave New York, she says, 'Later he made a painting inspired by that long dark night of the soul, as he thought of it: *The Rising*, probably the rawest of what I regarded as his phallic paintings' (47). Later, she describes how in his paintings he 'practically *violated* [the canvas], as he discharged rage with an energy which translated in the finished work as passion, and imbued it with considerable force' (135).

The story of Jack is a narrative of decentring, a decentring of the construct of the mythopoeic modernist – and male – artist. Gender plays a significant role in McGrath's novel. Jack's story has a female narrator and Gin bears, in some respects, an uncanny likeness to another significant Modernist figure: Virginia Woolf – but this is a Virginia Woolf who is artistically barren.[32] Like Woolf, Gin (Virginia) is, as she describes herself, 'a tall, thin, untidy Englishwoman' (12); her establishment of a room of her own (the New York brownstone), however, does no more than allow her a vicarious existence as a reader, in which, as she says, 'Jack was never far from my thoughts, nor absent from my innermost heart' (58). For Gin does exactly what Woolf recognizes other woman as having done down the ages: she serves as a 'looking glass possessing the magic and delicious power of reflecting man as twice his natural size'.[23] When she and Jack were both art students in London, she recognized, she claims, 'that he was a far better artist than I would ever be' (3), thus internalizing the androcentric view of art propounded by the offensive William Bankes to Lily Briscoe in *To the Lighthouse*, 'Women can't paint, women can't write'.[24]

The story of the novel, told through Gin's eyes, is as much an account of Gin's relationship with her brother as it is the story of Jack Rathbone and Vera Savage. Competing versions of the events in Port Mungo still stand by the end of the novel, although the reader comes to see the symbolic import of Vera's name – savage truth or truly wild, depending on how you translate it. Gin's identity is constructed entirely in relation to Jack. This is a quintessentially Gothic relationship, in which Gin acts as a kind of voyeur in Jack's life. As William Patrick Day suggests:

> The act of observing another person, often, though not always, secretly is a paradigmatic Gothic motif; it is the act of watching one's self. The characters' experience of watching their own doubles or projections is duplicated in the readers' relationship to the text. The act of reading is itself essentially voyeuristic, for the spectacle of Gothic sadomasochism and horror is an externalized, public, and thus mediated, expression of the reader's fears and desires.[25]

If she is one version of Jack's double, it is as a photographic negative to the image of the wild and assertive artist. Early on in her account she says, 'the most remarkable event of my life has been Jack himself! He travelled more than I did, he accomplished more, and he certainly suffered more – in short he had more memories than me' (12). Vera is the other doubled figure, the female artist who struggles for self-definition but at the end of the novel remains a working artist and is acknowledged as such by Gin:

all at once I understood why Vera wandered, and with that realization my moral understanding of the household tipped on its head and I saw Jack's formidable discipline as a kind of silent brooding ingrown negative energy which must have sapped the vitality of a woman like Vera and driven her wild with frustration. (84)

For much of the narrative, Gin insists on telling the reader that she believes Vera to be 'no good' (73), a reiteration of her first impression of this

loud bosomy woman in a tight dress and pancake make-up, one hand cocked akimbo on her hip and the other flapping the air as she spoke to us with a kind of hoarse nervous bravado ... Her hair was the colour of coal, her lips were scarlet and she had lost a tooth, whose absence lent her a distinctly menacing aspect when she grinned. (24)

She remembers 'thinking her opinionated and not very clean, nor entirely sober' (24). Vera passionately states her commitment to art in her encounter with the London art students, and a Gothic identity is hinted at by the location of her studio: 'a disused operating theatre in the basement of an old fever hospital' (24). Yet, while the reader knows much about Jack's paintings from frequent descriptions from Gin, Vera's paintings, her art, remain beyond the scope of vision in the novel.

In a recent article, Magali Falco reads the landscapes of the novel as 'an internal Narcissistic journey of the artist from the English urban landscape through the American urban jungle that will end in the primitive setting of Port Mungo, the heart of darkness'.[26] This is a tempting reading of a novel that offers up to the reader a now familiar Freudian textual landscape. The novel, however, resists such an inward voyage. What it eschews is depth; it is itself a version of the reflecting pool. Such a reading involves an acceptance of a mythopoeic representation of the modernist artist, which the novel actually seems to be questioning. As Michael Bell has observed in his study of literature, modernism and myth: 'Rather than modern man being able to recover the mythopoeic relation to nature and the self proposed by Cassirer and others, it is necessary to see that this conception was itself a myth, an unconscious example of modern mythopoeia.'[27] Jack's *Narcissus in the Jungle* comes to be seen by

Gin as a self-portrait and a reiteration of an old myth. Her view of Vera becomes moderated by her understanding of Jack's self-absorption: 'No wonder they fought! No wonder she left home for months on end, and took lovers, how else could she live with my brother, whose single conversation in life – and this I had already seen for myself – was with himself?' (84). His final painting, for which his daughter Anna has been sitting, is described by Vera as 'haunting', and Gin repeats and reflects:

> Haunting. Portrait of the artist as a young man . . . She was right, it was Jack as a boy. I had seen that thin white body often enough. It was Jack at seventeen, as he was when he first met Vera. He paints himself over and over again, I thought, it's all he ever does. Even his jungles are self-portraits, he told me so himself. (203)

Through the tropes of Gothic the novel throws into relief its cliché-ridden representation of the mythopoeic modernist artist, who is ultimately shown to be reiterating the old myth of Narcissus in his work. The truth-telling portrait, for example, has been a familiar feature of Gothic fiction, from Walpole onwards. Jack's corpse, discovered alongside this last portrait, is reminiscent of the closing lines of Oscar Wilde's *The Picture of Dorian Gray*. Recent work has challenged the orthodox view that the archaism of Gothic had no place in modernism. As Andrew Smith has pointed out, 'The influence of the Gothic on the modernist imagination is clear . . . this presence can be explained in terms of how Gothic images of damaged subjectivity and physical deformity echo anxieties relating to the post First World War period.'[28] But in McGrath's twenty-first-century novel about a mid to late twentieth-century artist, the time gap is important. Jack Rathbone is not an artist of the modernist period; he is acting out a myth forged, not in 'the smithy of [his] soul' (to use Joyce's words), but by others in an earlier period.[29] Even the suicide of this 'latter day Gauguin', in echoing that of Rothko, has, in Gin's words, 'a derivative quality to it' (241). If Michael Bell is right in saying that the conception of the mythopoeic artist was itself a myth, then McGrath's exposure of this truth means that the Gothic of the text has a different function from Gothicism in modernist texts. The Gothic tropes that haunt this novel provide a different narrative of the artist. Although McGrath is reluctant to identify this novel as a Gothic novel,[30] horror, madness, monstrosity, death, disease, terror, evil and weird sexuality – those characteristics of 'the New Gothic' – are all present in *Port Mungo* in full measure, as well as some conventional props of the genre. If *Port Mungo* is not consciously Gothic, then Gothic has effectively haunted its author. The signs are there early on. Gin's lengthy reflection on Jack's hands in the opening pages of the novel, for example, signal a metonymic emphasis that echoes other Gothic texts, one that McGrath had used in his early fiction. 'I saw what the years in Port Mungo had done to his hands', says Gin, commenting on the deformation of Jack's hands by arthritis (2). 'I have perfectly healthy hands, in fact my hands are my best thing. I used to say to Jack that if there were some way of making a hand exchange, I would do it at once' (12–13).

Jack himself has vampiric qualities in the way he drains others. There is a clear visual pointer to this in a disturbing scene from Peg's childhood:

> He sucked lustily at the dirty foot, sucked and spat, and every few seconds he lifted his eyes and grinned at her . . . After a minute or two, he sat back, picked at her foot with a fingernail, then extracted the thorn with his teeth. He held it up for us to see, then tossed it over the railing and wiped his hands on his paint-smeared trousers . . . before she limped off he had her stand with her back to the railing and urinated on her foot. To disinfect it, he said. (81)

Gin's response to this scene (which she witnesses) is to reflect on how far Jack had moved from 'civilized' behaviour, but it also provides a vivid metaphor for Jack's familial relationships. Back in New York, painting in the attic, Jack is perceived by Gin as 'one of the undead, the ghoul who made art in the attic' (190). Doubling is also present: Gin and Jack; Jack and Vera; Peg and Anna. Anna, as the double of Peg, acts as a revenant who brings about Jack's nemesis. As Gin reflects: 'Anna Rathbone by coming into our life like this, and rousing the past, was rousing her sister; and Peg, once roused, invariably laid waste to that most fragile of organs, I mean her father's heart' (124). Anna cuts a Gothic figure, with her bad British teeth: ' a glimpse of those yellow tombstone teeth. Like a death's head, I thought later' (185). When she leaves the brownstone for a while, Gin wonders:

'But for this – what? – this simulacrum, this *ghost*? – to die, figuratively – what did this mean? How could a ghost die? What did it mean to talk about the death of a ghost?' (210). The family secret of incest, a staple of Gothic fiction, is no longer unspeakable for the twenty-first-century reader, and it comes as no surprise. Jack's corpse beside his portrait of his daughter, which is also his self-portrait, provides a Gothic mise-en-scène that signals Jack's final decentring.

By the end, Vera emerges as the strongest figure, the one left intact in spite of her relationship with Jack. Her strength is acknowledged by Gin: 'In time I came to regard her differently, and even grew to like her; and after Jack's death I leaned on her heavily, when for a while she was the sole pillar of strength in a house of shattered women' (40). Through Gin's changing perceptions of Vera there comes an intimation of another image of the artist, whose relationship with the landscape rejects the Gothic of narcissism:

> Instead of the restless irresponsible creature he had described I saw a woman with a genuine curiosity about the world beyond this obscure little river town, and it was an artist's curiosity because it was as an artist that she spoke about what she'd seen ... I am a woman who likes to sit in a room in a city – preferably New York City – with a book in my hand and travel in my own imagination. So what Vera did, what she had been doing for years, was impressive to me. (83–4)

What she knows, what she has seen and what she paints, however remain beyond the scope of representation in the novel. Although very different from Stella Raphael, she, too, remains ultimately inaccessible.

By this point in McGrath's career, female figures had become very important. His next work, the trilogy of short stories set in New York at different points in its history, creates memorable female characters, and the figure of the mother assumes particular importance. The heroic mother-figure in the first, reminiscent of Martha Peake (with the same stature and startling red hair), is accessible only through the narrative of her guilt-ridden son, writing across the decades. The other two stories, however, are told by female narrators. In them, the artist and the doctor figures reappear and are further redefined, this time in relation to American history.

Ghost Town: Tales of Manhattan Then and Now (2005)

This set of linked short stories was written in response to an invitation from the publisher Bloomsbury to contribute a volume to their 'Writers and the City' series. McGrath chose to write fiction, 'three stories set in different centuries, a sort of urban archaeology',[31] his way of engaging with a violent history that had become all too present in the shadow of the events of 11 September 2001. As he remarked in an interview for the *Guardian*, 'Lower Manhattan has been fought over for centuries. It is one of the most violently contested pieces of real estate in history. And 9/11 is a part of that history.'[32] Moreover, as Todd McEwen in the *Guardian* perceptively commented:

> The military-industrial-entertainment behemoth has eclipsed any American ability to look to its political roots – yet, most intriguingly, this is what McGrath is doing: reminding us that America was born in violence, in terrorist actions that were deemed to be in a just cause.[33]

In this timely collection of stories, therefore, his Manhattan is haunted by history. As in *Port Mungo*, it is a liminal space. The fiction brings together personal and political histories and yet again, in spite of his resistance to being labelled as a Gothic novelist, Gothic gives shape to the occluded history of violence that has made Manhattan the place that it is. In all three, parental figures are used as a way of representing aspects of the American inheritance. The Gothic quality of the stories was noted by the reviewers; indeed, the *New York Times* review was subtitled 'Gothic Gotham'.[34]

McGrath himself acknowledges that each of the stories involves a ghost, but the nature of that ghost changes with the period. Speaking in 2006 he commented:

> Well that one, *The Year of the Gibbet*, was certainly a nakedly gothic tale. I found when I was on to the second story in this collection that I'd somehow got a ghost in each, but the nature of the ghost had changed over time. The first featured a very gothic one – a good old-fashioned, rotting, smelly creature, who appears to sharpen the guilt of some poor haunted man. Maybe there is a thesis on how the ghosts

we experience in the twenty-first century differ from those of the eighteenth century . . .[35]

In the image of the ghost, what is perhaps the most fundamental boundary of all is transgressed: that between life and death. Implied in this is a disruption of the linearity of time, and hence the undermining of the very dimension through which human beings define their mortality. In the words of Peter Buse and Andrew Stott: 'In the figure of the ghost, we see that past and present cannot be neatly separated from one another, as any idea of the present is always constituted through the difference and deferral of the past as well as the anticipations of the future.'[36] Each tale is set at a different key point in Manhattan's history, which McGrath uses as a cue to adopt the Gothic conventions and preoccupations of the time: a literary haunting is also at work. Figures and tropes now familiar from his earlier fiction are contextualized anew, so that the overlapping chronotopes that make up the whole of the trilogy become also a palimpsest of his own literary history.

His central figures are peripheral and powerless in relation to historical events: the first is a child; the second (whose story is narrated by a descendant of his sister) spends twenty years locked away in an asylum; and the third is a psychiatrist who experiences trauma at third hand and comes to believe in evil. The opening tale, 'The Year of the Gibbet', is perhaps closest to the lost dream of American innocence, although that innocence is called into question by the events of the story. Its narrator tells the reader: 'I can still recall an innocent time when Manhattan was a place of farms and tranquil orchards and it was said that visitors *smelled* the island even as their vessels came beating through the Narrows, our wild farms and fruit trees.'[37] As in *Spider* and *Asylum*, therefore, the archetypal image of the garden figures as a place of despoliation in which transgression and decay can do their worst, but which remains in the imagination as a place of lost delight. The nameless narrator tells a story of a child's perspective on some of the events of Revolutionary War, in which history and Gothic symbolism are entwined. As he speaks, it is 1832 and he is surrounded by death, as New York is in the grip of a cholera epidemic. He names the date: 'the Fourth of July', thus setting the scene for his tale of fifty-five years earlier. This is 1777, named 'The Year of the Gibbet', as he tells the reader: 'those three grim sevens, an invisible noose dangling from each of those crossbars, and a busy year for the gibbet it would prove to be' (31). Independence Day is no occasion for fireworks and celebration in this tale of American independence: this is a story about the price of independence, of betrayal and haunting guilt. The narrator has his mother's skull on the table before him, he tells the reader, a gruesome memento mori, which is translated before the tale ends into a ghost of abject corporeality. He has been haunted by his mother's ghost for the last fifty-five years ('I have never been free of my mama') and he realizes that his life has been dominated by a desire for death: 'I pursued my dead mama not because I wanted to *release* her from her coffin, but because I wanted to be *in* her coffin *with her*' (61). The close of the tale shows her ghost, as he sees it, in the abject form of a corpse beckoning him to his own death:

> She stands in the doorway with her empty eyes, her soiled clothing open at the seams and her teeth loose in her skull. The noisome odour of the grave is strong upon her. She lifts her pulpy rotten fingers, and in the street below I hear the death-cart rumble over the cobblestones and come to a halt outside the house. (62)

This a ghost that leaves nothing to the imagination, embodying in spectral form the death wish of the narrator.

His story describes the upheavals of the Revolutionary War from a child's perspective. Referring to the fleet anchored in Lower Bay, he says, 'I damn near fouled my britches when my brother Dan told they were King George's ships and had come with their cannon to blow us all to smithereens!' (5). He tells of his father returning from the Battle of Brooklyn and describing the bloody rout of Washington's soldiers; this is the last he saw of him, learning later that he had died of fever at Valley Forge. 'My mama', he says, 'was the only safe and stable element in this upside-down world' (8). The relationship between son and mother is central to this tale, in which the family endures privations and tragedy, along with the other people of Manhattan. The resourcefulness and bravery of this woman – like Martha Peake, a heroine of the Revolution and similar in appearance and temperament to her – is presented as emblematic of the New World; recalled as working 'from dawn to dusk' and bearing 'child after child', she is idolized by her son, who calls her 'a true patriot'. This woman (nameless like the narrator) is described by him as a 'proud strong woman', 'a tall proud woman', with 'a great mass of auburn hair', 'a big, handsome woman with broad shoulders and a thrusting chin, her neck a column of flesh the colour of marble − '. He then adds, 'But let me not speak of her neck' (8). This is a sign to the reader of what is to come later in the tale: her execution.

The confrontation between the heroic mother − the embodiment of American dreams of self-sufficiency and freedom − and the decadent English commander (his body bearing vampiric traces, with his skin 'white as chalk' and his lips 'scarlet' (11)) is the pivotal moment in the tale. He is represented as an avatar of death; with 'a large curved nose which resembled the blade of a scythe', he is a version of the grim reaper. After the town is fired (possibly by the revolutionaries, to prevent the King's men quartering there over the winter) and the family made homeless, she confronts Lord John Hyde, calling him 'a painted whore' and 'king's strumpet' (18). Instead of riding her down and whipping her, as he seems inclined to do, he holds back and his revenge is reserved for later, which comes when the mother and children are challenged on their return from Newark. The narrator recalls how he had faltered in his account of the reasons for their journey and then spent the rest of his life tormented by the belief that he had aroused the officer's suspicions. What ensues, he says, was '*all my fault*' (38). In her second meeting with Lord Hyde, brought before him, his mother is made to undress in full view of her children and of men with their faces 'pressed to the window'. The mother's pride remains intact, 'she showed no shame at all', and she lets down her auburn hair so that it covers her nakedness and exposes Hyde's lechery (42). A letter is discovered in her garments that incriminates her in an act of treason, a charge she denies with the retort, 'if guilt is to fight you butchers on my own soil', repudiating the authority of the court, on the grounds that she is a citizen of the United States of America (43). She is condemned to death and hanged by Lord Hyde in person, defiant until the end.

This female hero of the Revolution, in her form as a revenant,[38] signifies the burden of guilt carried by subsequent generations, a burden generated in the compromises and betrayals attendant on the violent making of the new nation. Blamed by his sister and brother, the narrator carries that burden of guilt throughout his life. In the 'present' time of the tale, New York 'has become a place not so much of death as of the *terror* of death' (1) – just as it was to become in 2001. He watches some women and children set out for Long Island in a small boat, apparently an attempt to escape the contagion, and he muses that their quest is in vain 'for wherever man goes, there goes the Pest' (2). The myth of the Revolution, he reflects, has become entrenched in the preceding fifty-five years, so that 'it now resembles nothing so much as the glorious enterprise of a small host of heroes and martyrs sustained by the idea of Liberty and bound for that reason to prevail in the end' (61). He knows, however, that 'the shores of Manhattan' are haunted by his 'mama', and although his end is near, that haunting returns in the subsequent two stories in different forms.

The second tale of the trilogy, 'Julius', visits Manhattan in the mid nineteenth century. The narrative voice is more distanced from the action in this tale, which is told by a female descendant of one of the protagonists. Not directly involved in the events of the tale, she has 'painstakingly assembled [them] by means of the fading memories of those who knew him' (173) and in time has come to realize that hers 'was not the only family in which violence and insanity had erupted in generations past and plagued the lives of those to come' (172). Uncovered in a leisurely manner as the unfolding of a mystery,[39] it is a tale of patriarchal oppression and dynastic self-interest in a period when the commercial class was consolidating its wealth and the city was growing at a rapid pace, in 'the din and turmoil of construction' (97). The familiar McGrath themes of love, madness and art – with their underlying intimations of transgression and decay – are interwoven in this tale of familial violence and its repercussions. The violence of the larger stage (the Civil War takes place during the period it covers) is incidental to its plot, but connected at a deeper level.

The opening both provides a Gothic frame and hints at the nature of the ghosts that haunts the tale. The ancestral portrait of Noah van Horn, inherited by his descendant, the narrator, gives form to madness-inducing patriarchal cruelty: the narrator sees in it a man who must have been 'bullish, loud, domineering, impatient', one who 'seems literally about to burst from the canvas and lay about one with a stick' (63). Another portrait, that of van Horn's son-in-law, is explicitly described by the narrator as 'a phantom', 'a human spirit preserved in oils' (155). Hence, the role of the painter is rendered uncanny in this tale, in which a painter – and what becomes of him – is central to the plot. The narrator envisages a family group at dinner:

> At the head of the table a syphilitic robber-baron flanked by a one-eyed painter and a man just out of an insane asylum, this damaged trio supported by the sisters, who . . . gave the faltering masculine energies in the room some ballast of civilized structure. (155–6)

The events that have led up to this scene constitute a family history of material success (which is not to be sustained into the narrator's time), but also of violence and insanity. Whereas the focal relationship in 'The Year of the Gibbet' is that of mother and son, a father's cruelty to his son is central in 'Julius'. The young Julius had been regularly beaten by his father 'for the smallest infractions of the rules of the household', to the extent that on one occasion he 'emerged weeping from his father's library . . . with blood running down his legs' (66–7). At this point the daughters (who are considerably older than their brother) had intervened and insisted that the beatings stop. The oldest, Charlotte, had told her father that 'the boy could not help it that he was what he was', causing him to see his own behaviour in a new light. The cause of his mother's death in childbirth, Julius is both a longed-for son and a disappointment; his father's punishment of him is an expression of his frustration that this is no suitable heir to 'the House of van Horn' (71).

Reconciled to his son's nature as he grows older – his innumeracy and lack of organization – Noah van Horn seeks out another young man to groom as his successor. This is Max Rinder, an ambitious young man of the kind common in New York at the time, who in time marries Charlotte and becomes the 'syphilitic robber-baron' (thus suffering terminally from the ailment that Ibsen addressed as one of the unspeakable family secrets in his play *Ghosts* (1898)). The van Horn dynasty's wealth is founded on violence, Noah's fortune being built on 'the Atlantic trade, running raw cotton out of Savannah, Georgia, carrying it to London then working his way down the eastern seaboard, turning a profit in every port' (64) – in other words, this is a fortune built on slavery. The familial violence, therefore, echoes a social violence that emerges later in the text as a historical event represented as incidental to the plot: the American Civil War, which takes place during the twenty-year period in which Julius is sequestered in a private asylum in the Hudson Valley. He is a man 'innocent of history', spared, as the narrator says, 'not only the war but the draft riots of July, 1863 when for days New York was under the control of a howling mob and all the family trembled for their lives' (154).

The events leading up to his incarceration involve another irruption of violence. With Charlotte's encouragement, Julius starts to develop his artistic talents under the tutelage of a landscape painter, Jerome Brook Franklin, and becomes infatuated with the life model, Annie Kelly. When Noah discovers that his son is in love with her, he charges Rinder with making her disappear. In this act, he is displaying the prejudices of the bourgeoisie: he is dismayed by both her social class and her origins, having already displayed his contempt for the Irish by deeming them to be the source of diseases that flourished in 'the narrow filthy streets and fetid courtyards where they lived' (65). Julius, however, suspects the painter and becomes possessed by a delusional madness. There are hints here of another kind of haunting, another kind of ghost. Distraught at the disappearance of Annie, he wanders the streets and returns, telling the butler 'that he had been out looking for his *mother*' (130). Although Julius's mother died when he was born and is therefore absent, as mothers often are in Gothic fiction, this lapse on his part may be read not only as portending psychological disturbance, but also as a signifier in the larger patterning of this trio of stories. Whereas the dead mother has an all too visible presence in 'The Year of the Gibbet', Julius's mother haunts this text as an absence. The masculine ascendancy of the mercantile classes, as exemplified by his family, leads to its own kind of violence and subsequent haunting.

Julius is put in the care of a doctor, who drugs him, and he is tended by his sisters, who claimed 'till the end of their days' that they saw something in Julius's bed that day: 'A *creature* . . . and there was a smell too, a strong smell, which they associated with raw meat and stables, and something else they could not identify, something quite horrid' (133). In the belief that Franklin is responsible for Annie's disappearance, Julius (now transformed into an abject creature, at least in the minds of his sisters) attacks the painter, gouging out his eye, in an act of symbolic castration, and changing his destiny as an artist in one blow. Julius's story lends itself well to a theoretical reading based on the psychoanalytic theory of cryptonomy. As in *Spider*, a deep hurt is buried, only to irrupt at a later point. As the narrator says, although he had seemed unperturbed by his father's brutality, 'Julius buried his pain, buried it so deep that no-one saw it not even himself' (83). As he is led away to the asylum, Noah, 'once the master of a great commercial empire', is 'now a broken old man' and dies within a year, leaving Rinder with control of his fortune (142). It is not just Brook Franklin who suffers from the emergence of the 'creature', therefore; the violence of van Horn has rebounded on himself. Julius's period in the asylum, a benign institution under the control of an 'alienist' (as such doctors were then called), is in keeping with ideas of the day about the nature and treatment of insanity. Its location is an irony not lost on the narrator, who, she reveals, is the grand-daughter of Brook Franklin and Sarah, the youngest of the van Horn sisters. Julius has spent twenty years in the Catskills, where the young Brook Franklin had painted and dreamed of helping to create an artistic tradition for a new nation, one 'which reflected its own true spirit, and the true spirit of America lay in the vast sublimities of her boundless unspoiled wilderness' (75). This is the landscape of Harry Peake in 'The American Within'. Brook Franklin's partial blinding at the hand of Julius destroys his capacity to achieve his dream. Instead, he becomes a portrait painter, able to profit from the aspirations of a rising middle class:

> Jerome Brook Franklin applied himself conscientiously to the work of portraiture, and in time he prospered, earning an income far greater than what he could have expected from landscape painting. But he had lost the work which had once answered every deep yearning of his painter's soul, I mean the depiction of the great natural vistas of the American wilderness. (144)

He becomes in later life an embittered alcoholic, having lost every-thing, and yet by the end of the tale he reveals his part in Julius's tragedy more fully: 'Yes, I ruined his life, and he ruined mine. The girl belonged to me, you see, and it was too much for him!' (172). Thus, Brook Franklin is not simply the innocent victim of a young

man's insanity but partly responsible for the tragedy that comprom-
ised his artistic vision. The story of Julius, therefore, is a complex
Gothic rendition of the reverberation of violence that has tainted
the vision of freedom that is 'America' itself. The female narrator
hints darkly at 'what I became' (her mother would have disapproved)
and implies tragedy in her own life. However, in piecing together
Julius's story from textual evidence, itself a kind of haunting (she refers
to 'the daguerreotypes, the photographs, the paintings' as 'phantoms,
merely'), she is able to derive a lesson, 'that love denied will make us
mad' (173). Hence, the Gothic trope of the family secret holds the
key to another stage in Manhattan's history.

The last tale of this trio is set in 2001, in the weeks after 9/11.
This event is already historic, like the War of Independence and the
Civil War; the reaching import of what happened was not lost on
those involved, nor on the rest of the world, who watched the planes
fly into the Twin Towers on their television screens. Only now are
writers and film-makers beginning to assimilate and represent this
traumatic moment in the history of America, New York and more
specifically Manhattan. In placing his tale alongside the two earlier
ones in the volume, McGrath emphasizes the threads of continuity
in the violence that has shaped and continues to shape this 'violently
contested piece of real estate'.[40]

This time he chooses a psychiatrist for his narrator; for those familiar
with McGrath's work, this is a warning sign. This psychiatrist is a
woman, 'a childless woman who never married', but one who regards
her patient, lawyer Danny Silver, as being 'like a son'. Danny's problems
are 'largely sexual in nature, and . . . originated in a suffocating maternal
relationship which created conflicts that ran like fault lines deep in
his psyche, becoming visible only when he tried to sustain intimacy
with a woman', she explains (175). Thus, the image of the mother
resurfaces in this tale both as a psychologically haunting presence
and through the surrogate relationship between doctor and patient.
The dynamic of the tale is carried by the changing perceptions of
the psychiatrist as she experiences vicariously the personal trauma
that many in the city have undergone. She moves away from the
certainties of the forensic approach of her profession, the approach
that leads her to say of Danny's lover, 'I could have tidied her up in a
couple of sessions, no great problem there, routine psychiatry' (186).

Instead, she comes to believe in evil: 'For my entire professional life, that is until I went down to Ground Zero, I had rejected the concept of evil. I had believed only in the impress of bad circumstances on the vulnerable mind' (231–2). In facing Ground Zero, she understands why Dan, in an echo of Eliot's *The Waste Land*, has called the city 'unreal' (187). She now inhabits a Gothic space. As she contemplates the 'Gothic remnant of the south tower', she recalls seeing a damaged underwear store on Broadway, in which 'a limbless, headless mannikin's torso clad in a skimpy red teddy dangles from a string, turning gently in the breeze', a grotesque echo of the fate of the heroic mother in 'The Year of the Gibbet' (239).

The tale entwines the historical with the personal, using the psychiatrist's account of Danny's relationship with the Chinese woman, Kim Lee, to explore the 'watershed' that is 11 September, 'after which everything seemed dark and tortured and incomprehensible' (212). The psychiatrist sees herself as 'engaged in terminal conflict with the prostitute Kim Lee, and the prize was Danny Silver's sanity' (215). In tracing its complex patterns of betrayal and guilt, this tale sets up two overlapping triangular relationships, with the artist/prostitute Kim Lee as their common link. Dan has become involved with Kim Lee after buying her services as a prostitute, a few days after 9/11. The relationship moves beyond business as he becomes drawn into her personal anguish, as she believes herself haunted by the ghost of her dead lover, who has perished in the Twin Towers. The reader's knowledge of her relationship with the lover, Jay Minkoff, is mediated several times over. The psychiatrist gives an account of Dan's version of the story Kim Lee has told him about her involvement with Jay. As the towers burned, she tells him, she had a last conversation with her lover in which he told her he loved her and that he was going to call his father to say goodbye, and then 'she stood there on her roof with her cell phone in her hand . . . trying to make out which of those distant falling people was her lover' (183). Later that day she had seen his ghost in the subway station, and it had looked at her with 'a terrible quiet sad anger . . . directed not at the men who had murdered him, but at her' (184). Dan understands that she feels responsible for his death, and speculates that this manifestation of her guilt 'did not merely materialize on the periphery of her consciousness, but that he was capable of states of feeling which directly affected her. He had agency' (185).

It is only in the later part of the tale that the full story of Jay and Kim Lee's relationship is gradually revealed. She had embarked on an affair with this 'rich kid', the son of 'a prominent New York banker and philanthropist' (216–17). He had taken her to meet his father, who, claiming interest in her artistic aspirations, had later visited her. They had sex and he paid her; 'the idea of fucking the father', Dan tells her, 'excited her' (225). This continues, and one day they 'get caught' (Dan speculates that they must have wanted to) as Jay walks in on them (236). At the psychiatrist's prompting, he concludes that the father must have hated his son. This family drama is framed by the narrator in terms of the greater calamity around them: 'The silence that follows. The stillness. The three figures frozen in space as they await the sickening impact of whatever it is that is coming towards them at unimaginable speed— ' (238).

The psychiatrist has already prompted Dan to acknowledge the parallel between Paul Minkoff (the father) and himself. Both have paid for a spurious intimacy with this woman. She has also elicited from him a statement that Kim Lee is 'the devil', but ignores the 'bitter irony' with which he says it and endorses this view of 'the devil who'd infatuated him' (234–5). This discourse represents the departure from the usual scientific discourse of the psychiatrist and is indicative of her own descent into a pathological state. She had delayed visiting Ground Zero, 'not wishing to be among a crowd of ghouls' (193), but it is through her that the direct description of the destruction comes. She is, she says, 'sick to my soul' as she contemplates 'the monumental shards of the towers' aluminium-faced columns with their slender Gothic arches', which make her think she is 'gazing at the wreckage of some vast modernist cathedral' (195). Thus, the *fin-de-siècle* decadence of the early tale 'The Angel', with its intimations of terminal modernist decline, reaches its culmination in this scene of destruction, which 'reeked of hatred and evil'. In this one powerful symbol, the resurgence of the dark forces of evil appears to the narrator, and her statement, 'I am a psychiatrist. I do not believe in evil, I believe all human experience can be traced to the impress of prior events upon the mind' (196), already seems to express a wavering conviction. Her battle for the 'sanity' of her patient therefore begins to take on a darker aspect. She becomes obsessive and paranoid about Kim Lee. She insists on seeing her, and makes Dan agree to bring her to a restaurant where she can observe her. Her reaction to the woman suggests an incipient xenophobia; she is surprised to see that she is Chinese, 'Or Asian anyway' (204). This racial suspicion is linked with a more public paranoia a few pages later, when she expresses her belief that John Ashcroft may be right in his 'ethnic profiling, the rounding up of as many men as they can find of near Eastern or North African descent. The suspension of due process, the wholesale pullback of traditional American freedoms — ' (212).[41] Thus, in the New York of September 2001, she makes of Kim Lee an abject figure, not quite human but identified as 'feline' with a 'vicious little face', one on to whose 'otherness' is abjected a multiplicity of negative feelings (205–6). Kim Lee stands in a Gothic tradition of such figures, like Svengali, Dracula and the Phantom of the Opera, whose racially inflected 'otherness' becomes a repository for that which cannot be accepted by dominant discourses, in this case the American discourses of justice and freedom.[42] She becomes, in short, 'the devil'. Whereas Dan insists on seeing her as an artist who does 'escort work to cover the rent on her loft' (181), the psychiatrist refers to her as a 'Chinese hooker' (209). There is no authoritative version of her in this tale; like Martha Peake, she is the product of a layered narrative. She is one in a line of artist figures in McGrath's fiction, and the one who is the most implicated in cultural betrayal.

At the end of the tale, Dan and Kim Lee are still together and he has discontinued his therapy. He has announced his intention to sell his dead mother's apartment, which he says is 'full of ghosts', and move in with her. The psychiatrist is convinced that she will suffocate him like his (bad) mother and return to her, the (good) mother surrogate ('I miss my big bear but I think he will come back to me when the affair collapses' (242)). Thus, in this last tale, the most recent violence of all is subtly linked with Manhattan's violent past, a past that is understood in terms of mothers and fathers. As the narrator of the first tale reflects:

> Everything finds its way across the Atlantic in the end. If our Pilgrim Fathers believed they had left the corruption of old Europe behind them, how wrong they have been proven! The corruption of old Europe – why, they brought it ashore at Plymouth Rock! I think in my mother's day we saw the last of the American effort to cleanse

ourselves of the stain of old Europe; certainly it was in this spirit she fought and died for the republic. (29)

This is far removed from the optimism of Harry Peake about the freshness of the New World. In *Ghost Town*, there is a recognition of the inescapability of history which is paralleled by the persistence of Gothic. Although protean in form, it continues to haunt McGrath's fictional representations of the city and its people.

4

Afterword:
Exorcizing the ghosts of the Gothic

ജരോ

McGrath's most recent novel, *Trauma*, was published in 2008. Speaking at the 2007 conference of the International Gothic Association, he stated that the scholars gathered there must be the ones to decide whether or not it could be described as Gothic. His reluctance to accept the label 'Gothic novelist' relates to anxieties of reception, perhaps even a residual suspicion that 'Gothic' remains a marginal genre, still anchored to the props of its earlier phases, however ironic-ally they might be engaged. The evolution of his writing has shown a development from a postmodern and playful engagement with these Gothic 'props' to an exploration into the darker recesses of the human mind and the effects of trauma on personal and public histories. In these later texts, traces of them remain, however. In McGrath's writing career, Gothic has not been contained in Drogo Hall.

Emerging out of this body of work are the twin figures of the artist and the psychiatrist, sometimes (as in *Asylum*) each other's double. Neither is innocent; their relationship with that which they attempt to represent and treat respectively is shown always to have a degree of complicity. Although McGrath's artists work in the visual medium, are sculptors like Edgar Stark or painters like Jack Rathbone, they represent a creativity that is analogous to that of the writer. As McGrath has said, 'they work in ways similar to writers. Jack Rathbone's anxiety and despair in front of a blank canvas is not unlike the writer's before a blank page, which makes such characters highly attractive in terms of a sort of veiled self-expression.' He echoes Cronenberg, who, when filming *Spider*, saw his central character as an artist rather than a madman (stating 'Spider c'est moi'), by adding (probably tongue in cheek), 'Edgar Stark, c'est moi'.[1] The exploration of artists' capacity for self-delusion and exploitation of their subjects is a continuing theme. The tendency of the psychiatrist to desire to control (at its most extreme, to own, as in the case of *Asylum*'s Peter Cleave) always undermines their claim to objectivity. Representing or decoding the darker depths of the human psyche cannot, it is suggested, ever be a disinterested and objective activity. Furthermore, it is intrinsically weird.

A perceptive review of *Trauma* (by Adam Mars Jones, in the *Observer*) identifies a long-standing conflict between literature and psychiatry:

> there exists a Hundred Years' War (a hundred years and counting) between literature and psychiatry, a territorial struggle in which no truce can hold for long. From the viewpoint of literature, psychiatry is an upstart and usurper, a cuckoo in the nest, but a cuckoo which wears a white coat, claiming the alien authority of science for its insights into human behaviour. And literature from the point of view of psychiatry? A bystander with first aid training at best, barely competent to keep the patient breathing until the specialists arrive on the scene.[2]

McGrath's work reflects the scepticism of the novelist about the 'alien authority of science'; his psychiatrists do not have the answers and are prone to suffer from disorders that they do not themselves recognize. The persistent image of the egotistical artist, however, also suggests limitations on his/her power to reveal the horrors that may lurk in the human psyche. In the case of Jack Rathbone, he can do no more than paint his own reflection over and over again.

McGrath's novels are peopled by dysfunctional characters and his complex narrations demand much of the reader. From *The Grotesque* onwards, the novels draw the reader into their own web of complex ambiguity. Their resistance to definitive closure means that the Gothic trace lingers; the power of suggestion makes for disquiet. Abject acts, such as the final moments of *Dr Haggard's Disease*, evoke powers of horror; the probing of the unstable boundary between sanity and madness shakes the props of identity in an unsettling way. The comfort of a containing medical explanation is denied. The later transatlantic fiction is also haunted by the Gothic. From the artful use of pastiche in *Martha Peake* to the vampiric discourse in *Port Mungo* and the spectral history of Manhattan, the Gothic sensibility persists. The preoccupation in much of this work with the making of America means not only that the unreliability of history is brought to the fore, but that the past is always Gothicized. It remains to haunt the present, as the linked tales of *Ghost Town* demonstrate. The descent of the psychiatrist narrator in 'Ground Zero' into paranoia and her growing conviction of the existence of evil, in the face of the public trauma of 9/11, is another step in challenging the authority of psychiatry.

Trauma is the most inward journey of all McGrath's fictions and the first one to be narrated by its protagonist since *Dr Haggard's Disease*. It is also a novel of New York, set for most of the time in the city during the dirty and dangerous period of the 1980s. The psychiatrist narrator of *Trauma*, Charlie Weir, is as troubled as his patients, among whom he has numbered Vietnam veterans who have witnessed and performed literally unspeakable atrocities, including (it is strongly hinted) breaking one of the most fundamental of taboos, that of cannibalism. The central trauma of the novel, however, is Charlie's, and the dynamic of the narrative brings it to a climactic moment when the source of that trauma and its significance for the other events of his life are brought into full consciousness for him. At that point, at the very end of the novel, he switches roles from doctor to patient. Divested of any of the jokiness of the earlier work and of many of the residual trappings of the Gothic, *Trauma* nonetheless deals with one of the key concerns of Gothic fiction: traumatic violence kept hidden even from the conscious self. In this respect, this is very much in the legacy of Poe, whose 'paranoids and neurotics', as the introduction to *The New Gothic* claims, '[blaze] a trail through the darkness that the greatest of his followers, the psychologist Freud, would explore in the creation of some of the most inspired tales in the genre, the chillingly macabre "case studies"' (xiv). In the words of one interviewer, 'put simply, McGrath has, over the course of his 20-year writing career, joined the dots between Poe and Freud'.[3]

Reviewers have been divided about the Gothic quality of this latest novel. According to the *Daily Telegraph*:

> In the best Gothic tradition, it is the promise of horror that keeps you reading . . . Yet the pleasure of the book is that of the detective as we sift through the layers of Charlie's self-deception and false memories to get to the real image of our narrator as a broken man, tormented by desires he can't control. Fans of McGrath's dark world will be in ecstasies; those hoping for a new departure will be disappointed.[4]

Adam Mars Jones, however, has a different take, suggesting that although 'Patrick McGrath's fiction has always concerned itself with the dark places of the mind . . . the emphasis has shifted':

> *Trauma*, though a very expert literary novel, is structured more or less as a thriller and, like most thrillers, its big finale brings with it a certain sense of letdown. This is not a comment on Patrick McGrath's level of accomplishment but on the workings of genre. When the bogeyman who has haunted our lives is coaxed into the open by a supportive therapist and shown to be powerless, the sense of disappointment is part of the breakthrough . . . But when in a story the secret comes into the open and is seen for what it is, we usually want our money back, unless we are compensated with an image that can continue to haunt us.[5]

Where *Trauma* departs from Poe's legacy is in bringing to light the source of the trauma and in its implication that therapy might indeed be able to address it. At the end of the novel its desperate narrator, who has had the source of his own trauma revealed to him by his artist brother, returns to the mental hospital (a Victorian asylum in the Catskills) where he has been working as a doctor, and puts himself in the hands of a woman psychiatrist.

In spite of the Gothic themes of *Trauma*, in which transgression and decay are present in multiple guises, this novel represents what seems to be a conscious attempt to move away from the Gothic, to exorcize the ghosts of the Gothic. In Gothic, deeper darker secrets (either personal or cultural) are displaced on to the spectral or abject. Here, the source of Charlie's problems is eventually revealed and the displacement he has engaged in for the whole of his adult life is shown to stem from a deeply traumatic incident with his mother when he was six. As McGrath told Nicholas Wroe, 'Early in my research I talked to a psychiatrist who said "it's the mothers" that make us go into this line of work.'[6] *Trauma* appears to bring into the light what Anne Williams refers to as the 'nightmère';[7] the novel's imbrication with the legacy of the Vietnam War and the symbolic power of the mother in the earlier works suggest, however, that the Gothic is not entirely exorcized and, like the undead, may well return in McGrath's future work.

Notes

ಬಿಂ

Introduction

1. Anecdote related by Patrick McGrath in an address to the International Gothic Association, 18 July 2003.

2. 'The labelling as a Gothic writer in his early career did become problematic, and he complains that it encouraged people not to read the books attentively because "they think they know what's going on before they start. Certainly in something like *The Grotesque*, and even in *Martha Peake*, I was being very deliberately Gothic. In other books I thought I was trying to fry different fish." That said, he remains fascinated with the gothic literature that preceded Freud and is constantly delighted by "insights into the mind that are constantly in evidence despite the absence of Freudian theory".' Interview with Nicholas Wroe, *Guardian*, 12 July 2008. Available on-line at *http://www.guardian.co.uk/books/2008/jul/12/saturdayreviewsfeatres.guardianreview19* (accessed 26 February 2009).

3. Daphne du Maurier, Introduction by Patrick McGrath, *Don't Look Now: Selected Stories of Daphne du Maurier* (New York: Random House, 2008).

4. Philip Hensher, Review of *Martha Peake*, *Observer*, 20 August 2000. Available on-line at *http://www.guardian.co.uk/books/2000/aug/20/fiction.reviews3* (accessed 26 February 2009).

5. Patrick McGrath, 'Transgression and Decay', in Cristoph Grunenberg (ed.), *Gothic: Transmutations of Horror in Late Twentieth-Century Art* (Cambridge, MA: MIT Press, 1997), pp. 158–3. (The pagination runs backwards in this volume.)

6. Ibid., p. 153.

7. For some time during the 1990s, there were debates about the use of the term and some critics lamented the emerging looser definitions that released 'Gothic' from its moorings in late eighteenth-century fiction. See, for example, Maurice Lévy, '"Gothic" and the critical idiom', in Allan Lloyd Smith and Victor Sage

(eds), *Gothick Origins and Innovations* (Amsterdam: Rodopi Press, 1994), pp. 1–15.

8   Fred Botting (ed.), *The Gothic* (Cambridge: Brewer, 2001), p. 1.

9   See, for example, Robert Miles: 'The Gothic may evince no single dialectic, but there is broad agreement that the Gothic represents the subject in a state of deracination, of the self finding itself dispossessed in its own house, in a condition of rupture, disjunction, fragmentation.' (Robert Miles, *Gothic Writing 1750–1820*, 2nd edition (Manchester: Manchester University Press, 2002), p. 3).

10   For an exploration of boundaries and thresholds at different levels in Gothic fiction, see Manuel Aguirre, 'Narrative structure, liminality, self-similarity: the case of Gothic fiction', in Isabel Soto (ed.), *A Place that is Not a Place: Essays in Liminality and Text* (Madrid: Gateway Press, 2000), pp. 134–51.

11   Richard Davenport-Hines, *Gothic: 400 Years of Excess, Horror, Evil and Ruin* (London: Fourth Estate, 1998), p. 378.

12   Patrick McGrath, interview with Magali Falco, 5 July 2003. In Magali Falco, *A Collection of Interviews with Patrick McGrath* (Paris: Éditions Publibook, 2007), p. 32.

13   Ibid., p. 26.

14   Bradford Morrow and Patrick McGrath (eds), *The New Gothic* (New York: Random House, 1991), p. xi. Page numbers hereafter in the text.

15   The growing interest in Gothic in the academy was signalled by the inaugural conference of what was to become the International Gothic Association in the same year. This body 'unites teachers, scholars, students, artists, writers and performers from around the world who are interested in any aspect of gothic culture: fiction, drama, poetry, art, film, music, architecture, popular culture and technology. It promotes the study and dissemination of information on gothic culture from the mid eighteenth century to the contemporary moment.' (International Gothic Association website: *http://www.iga.stir.ac.uk/index.php*, accessed 7 April 2010.)

16   Bradford Morrow and Patrick McGrath (eds), *The New Gothic: A Collection of Contemporary Gothic Fiction*, p. xiv.

17   McGrath recalls that King did him a great favour once, writing a glowing letter of support when McGrath was experiencing difficulty with USA immigration. (Interview with Peter Murphy, October 2008, at *http://wordpress.hotpress.com/petermurphy/2008/10/14/patrick-mcgrath-confessions-of-a-dangerous-mind/*, accessed 29 May 2009.)

18   See Simon Dentith, *Parody* (London: Routledge, 2000); Margaret Rose, *Parody: Ancient, Modern and Post-Modern* (Cambridge: Cambridge University Press, 1993); and Linda Hutcheon, *A Theory of Parody: The Teachings of Twentieth-Century Art Forms* (London: Methuen, 1985).

19   Patrick McGrath, interview with Magali Falco, 5 July 2003. In Falco, *Interviews with Patrick McGrath*, p. 32.

20   Chris Baldick, Introduction to *The Oxford Book of Gothic Tales* (Oxford: Oxford University Press, 1992), p. xxiii.

21 Hutcheon, *A Theory of Parody*, p. 6. See Umberto Eco's witty formulation of postmodern irony in 'Postmodernism, irony and the enjoyable', in Peter Brooker, *Modernism/Postmodernism* (Harlow: Longman, 1992).

22 Andrew Smith, *Gothic Literature* (Edinburgh: Edinburgh University Press, 2007), p. 141.

23 Allan Lloyd Smith, 'Postmodernism/Gothicism', in Victor Sage and Allan Lloyd Smith (eds), *Modern Gothic: A Reader* (Manchester: University Press, 1996), p. 18.

24 For example, McGrath says that names are very important to him but when it was suggested that 'Vincent Cushing' in *Dr Haggard's Disease* seemed a deliberate evocation of the world of horror cinema, he replied that he had named the character after the famous surgeon. (E-mail correspondence with the author, 28 February 2009.)

25 There is very little academic criticism of McGrath's fiction to date. The most substantial work is Magali Falco's book, *La Poétique néo-gothique de Patrick McGrath* (2007), which is not available in English and does not consider anything beyond the 2000 novel *Martha Peake*. Falco's work takes a psycho-analytic approach to these earlier novels.

26 Nicholas Royle, *The Uncanny* (Manchester: Manchester University Press, 2003), p. 2.

27 See, for example, Terry Castle, *The Female Thermometer: Eighteenth Century Culture and the Invention of the Uncanny* (Oxford: Oxford University Press, 1995).

28 Royle, *The Uncanny*, p. 206.

29 Julia Kristeva, *Powers of Horror: An Essay on Abjection*, trans. Leon S. Roudiez (New York: Columbia University Press, 1982), p. 4.

30 See Jerrold E. Hogle, 'The Gothic and the "otherings" of ascendant culture: the original *Phantom of the Opera*', in Glennis Byron and David Punter (eds), *Spectral Readings: Towards a Gothic Geography* (Basingstoke: Macmillan, 1999), pp. 177–201, and *The Undergrounds of The Phantom of the Opera: Sublimation and the Gothic in Leroux's Novel and its Progeny* (New York and Basingstoke: Palgrave Macmillan, 2002); and Robert Miles, 'Abjection, nationalism and the Gothic', in Fred Botting (ed.), *The Gothic* (Cambridge: D. S. Brewer, 2000), pp. 47–70.

31 Hogle, 'Gothic and the "otherings" of ascendant culture', p. 180.

32 David Punter, *The Literature of Terror, Vol. 2, The Modern Gothic*, 2nd edition (London: Longman, 1996), p. 125.

33 Chris Baldick and Robert Mighall, 'Gothic criticism', in David Punter (ed.), *A Companion to the Gothic* (Oxford: Blackwell, 2000), p. 209.

34 Anne Williams, *Art of Darkness: A Poetics of Gothic* (Chicago: University of Chicago Press, 1995), p. 242.

35 William Patrick Day, *In the Circles of Fear and Desire: A Study of Gothic Fantasy* (Chicago: University of Chicago Press, 1985), p. 179.

36 Alexandra Warwick, 'Victorian Gothic', in Catherine Spooner and Emma McEvoy, *The Routledge Companion to Gothic* (Oxford and New York: Routledge, 2007), pp. 29–37 (p. 36).

[37] McGrath's father was Dr Patrick McGrath, who was for many years super-intendant of Broadmoor, the high-security psychiatric hospital, where the young McGrath was brought up.

[38] McGrath uses this name again for an even more minor character in *Dr Haggard's Disease*.

[39] Interview with Nicholas Wroe, *Guardian*, 12 July 2008. *http://www.guardian.co.uk/books/2008/jul/12/saturdayreviewsfeatres.guardianreview19* (accessed 26 February 2009).

[40] He is happy to talk about his childhood and readily shares stories, such as that of the vicar who had baked his mother's head in the oven. Patrick McGrath, address to the conference of the International Gothic Association, Liverpool, 18 July 2003.

1. Playing with Gothic

[1] Patrick McGrath in an interview with Gilles Menegaldo, *Sources*, 5 (November, 1998), 109–27 (111).

[2] Patrick McGrath, 'Afterword: the new Gothic', in *Conjunctions*, 14 (Spring, 1990). Available on-line at *http://www.conjunctions.com/archives/c14-pm.htm* (accessed 5 July 2009).

[3] E-mail correspondence with the author, 18 February 2009. This story was reprinted in *The Year's Best Fantasy and Horror: Fifth Annual Collection*, ed. Ellen Datlow and Terri Windling (New York: St Martin's Press, 1992).

[4] There are echoes here of Charlotte Perkins Gilman's story 'The Yellow Wall-paper', where the heroine, who is in effect incarcerated in the attic of what may have been a home for the insane, begins to smell the wallpaper. In her case it is a 'yellow' smell and, in its evocation of the 'yellow' of babies' nappies, may be read as her repudiation of motherhood.

[5] Patrick McGrath, 'The Smell', in Bradford Morrow and Patrick McGrath, *The New Gothic* (pp. 239–48), p. 241.

[6] Eve Kosofsky Sedgwick, *The Coherence of Gothic Conventions* (1980; New York and London: Methuen, 1986), p. 7.

[7] Kelly Hurley, *The Gothic Body: Sexuality, Materialism, and Degeneration at the Fin de Siècle* (Cambridge: Cambridge University Press, 1996), pp. 3–4.

[8] Jerrold E. Hogle, 'The Gothic at the turn of the century: our culture of simulation and the return of the body', in Fred Botting (ed.), *The Gothic* (London: Brewer, 2000), p. 167.

[9] Ibid., p. 168.

[10] Bakhtin's term is used to denote the nexus between the principal temporal and spatial sequences of a work of art. 'From a narrative and compositional point of view, this is the place where encounters occur [. . . where] the webs of intrigue are spun, denouements occur and finally – this is where dialogues happen, something that acquires extraordinary importance in the novel,

revealing the character, "ideas" and "passions" of the heroes.' (M. M. Bakhtin, *The Dialogic Imagination: Four Essays*, ed. Michael Holquist, trans. Caryl Emerson and Michael Holquist (Austin: University of Texas Press, 1981), p. 250.)

11 *Blood and Water* (1988; Harmondsworth: Penguin Books, 1989), p. 70. Page numbers hereafter in the text.

12 See Colin Green, 'Back to school: a note on Patrick McGrath's "Ambrose Syme"', in *Peake Studies*, 1, 4 (Summer 1990), 5–8, for the influence of Mervyn Peake's work on the story.

13 See Victor Sage, *Horror Fiction in the Protestant Tradition* (Basingstoke and New York: Palgrave Macmillan, 1988).

14 Interview with Menegaldo, p. 113. McGrath cites Stevenson as a favourite author in an interview with Magali Falco, 5 July 2003. In Falco, *A Collection of Interviews with Patrick McGrath*, p. 32.

15 Interview with Falco, ibid.

16 The protagonist in this story bears names that appear elsewhere in McGrath's fiction. Evelyn is a marker of androgyny (perhaps echoing the 'he Evelyn' and 'she Evelyn' of Evelyn Waugh's first marriage) and is the real name of Neville Pilkington in 'The Skewer'. There are several Piker-Smiths in McGrath's fiction. They are distinguished by their ordinariness.

17 Lockwood's touching the ice-cold hand of Cathy's ghost, in Emily Brontë's *Wuthering Heights*, and Jekyll's awakening to find not his own but Hyde's hand on the coverlet, in Robert Louis Stevenson's *The Strange Case of Dr Jekyll and Mr Hyde*, are just two examples.

18 McGrath was to use this motif of removal from history in *Spider* (1990) and the short story 'Julius', in *Ghost Town* (2005), which both involve central characters who live sequestered through turbulent times, although in their case he makes their return to the mainstream of life a key dynamic in the plot.

19 Examples include Anne Rice's *Interview with the Vampire* (1976), Suzy McKee Charnas's *The Vampire Tapestry* (1980), Chelsea Quinn Yarbro's 'Saint-Germain' cycle of novels and stories (1978–2009), Poppy Z. Brite's *Lost Souls* (1992), and, more recently, the novels of Charlaine Harris ('Southern Vampire' series 2001–10 and ongoing) and Stephanie Meyer (*Twilight* (2005)), with their successful television and film adaptations.

20 Originally published as 'Cleave the Vampire or a Gothic Pastorale', in Michelle Slung, *I Shudder at Your Touch* (New York: New American Library, 1991), and retitled 'Not Cricket' in the British edition in the same year (Harmondsworth: Penguin, 1991), pp. 117–30. Page numbers hereafter in the text.

21 Wallop Hall is not as preposterous a name as it might sound – there are several villages in Hampshire with 'Wallop' in their names.

22 See Milly Williamson, *The Lure of the Vampire: Gender, Fiction and Fandom from Bram Stoker to Buffy* (London: Wallflower Press, 2005).

23 For an extended discussion of 'the comic turn' in Gothic fiction, see Horner and Zlosnik, *Gothic and the Comic Turn*; for a discussion of McGrath's comic Gothic writing in relation to masculinity, see pp. 145–66.

24   The very name of the house is a pun on 'flange', a protruding rim used to strengthen joints in plumbing. It also implies a play on a popular term for madness, 'unhinged', which is what Sir Norman becomes.

25   For a detailed reading of this story see Horner and Zlosnik, *Gothic and the Comic Turn* (pp. 150–3).

26   The historical Max Nordau was not a psychiatrist. In *Degeneration* (1892; published in England in 1895), a very influential book in its time, Nordau launched an attack on the degeneracy of contemporary art and culture and dismissed mysticism in any form as being the product of hysteria. There are similarities between McGrath's Max Nordau and his historical namesake: visions are dismissed as pathological, products of the diseased mind; mysticism is a symptom of degeneracy.

27   Interview with Menegaldo, p. 112.

28   William Patrick Day, *In the Circles of Fear and Desire: A Study of Gothic Fantasy* (Chicago: University of Chicago Press, 1985), p. 59.

29   McGrath appears to be parodying a familiar image from horror movies. *The Beast with Five Fingers* (1946), an adaptation of W. F. Harvey's 1928 tale, features the severed hand of a concert pianist, which wreaks havoc. The disembodied hand turns up in the comic Gothic film of *The Addams Family* (1991), in which 'Thing' is a member of the household and performs useful chores.

30   For two key essays on masturbation in Gothic fiction see Diane Mason, '"A very devil with the men": the pathology and iconography of the erotic consumptive and the attractive masturbator', in *Gothic Studies*, 2, 2 (August 2000), 205–17, and Robert Mighall, '"A pestilence which walketh in darkness": diagnosing the Victorian vampire', in Glennis Byron and David Punter (eds), *Spectral Readings: Towards a Gothic Geography* (Basingstoke and New York: Palgrave Macmillan, 1999) pp. 108–24.

31   For a more detailed reading of this story and its comic dimensions, see Horner and Zlosnik, *Gothic and the Comic Turn*, pp. 153–4.

32   Interview with Peter Murphy, 14 October 2008: *http://wordpress.hotpress.com/petermurphy/2008/10/14/patrick-mcgrath-confessions-of-a-dangerous-mind/* (accessed 29 May 2009).

33   Andrew Hock-Soon Ng, *Dimensions of Monstrosity in Contemporary Fiction* (Basingstoke: Palgrave Macmillan, 2004), p. 146.

34   Harry's name is very similar to that of the anti-heroine of Mary Elizabeth Braddon's 1862 novel *Lady Audley's Secret*, Helen Talboys. As well as evoking the melodramas of sensation fiction, this points to the theme of concealed identity, which is central to both Braddon's novel and McGrath's story.

35   See Kelly Hurley's analysis of the representation of entropic bodies at the end of the nineteenth century: 'a randomly working Nature is figured as too imaginative, *too* prolific. Any admixture of diverse morphic traits is possible, so that even highly complex bodies, ingeniously specialized for their environment … are abominable', *The Gothic Body: Sexuality, Materialism, and Degeneration at the Fin de Siècle* (Cambridge: Cambridge University Press, 1996), p. 9.

[36] Sigmund Freud, 'The Uncanny' (1919), in *Sigmund Freud: The Penguin Freud Library* (London: Penguin Books, 1985), vol. 14, 'Art and Literature', p. 345.

[37] Ibid., p. 148.

[38] See Introduction, n. 11.

[39] Barth's short story 'Lost in the Funhouse' (1968) may be regarded as seminal in its representation of fiction as play. Fowles had enjoyed enormous popularity in England and America, particularly through *The French Lieutenant's Woman* (1969) and its film adaptation (1981).

[40] Interview for BLDG Blog *http://bldgblog.blogspot.com/2007/07/possibility-of-secret-passageways.html* (accessed 3 August 2009).

[41] The connotations of the word 'ceck' are less obvious. There is a similarity to both 'cock' and the differently spelt 'kecks', Liverpool slang for trousers.

[42] Interview for BLDG Blog.

[43] Patrick McGrath, *The Grotesque* (1989; London: Penguin Books, 1990), p. 42. Page numbers hereafter in the text.

[44] Interview with Menegaldo, p. 112.

[45] Wolfgang Kayser, *The Grotesque in Art and Literature*, translated by Ulrich Weisstein (Bloomington: Indiana University Press, 1957), p. 21.

[46] See n. 33.

[47] Interview with Menegaldo, p. 115.

[48] For a detailed reading of the novel as comic Gothic, see Horner and Zlosnik, *Gothic and the Comic Turn*, pp. 155–64.

[49] Matthew Lewis, *The Monk* (1796; Oxford: Oxford University Press, 1995), p. 415.

[50] Allon White and Peter Stallybrass, *The Politics and Poetics of Transgression* (Ithaca: Cornell University Press, 1986), p. 51.

[51] Ibid., p. 44.

[52] Interview with Menegaldo, p. 115.

[53] 'So-called "homosexual panic" is the most private psychologized form in which many twentieth-century western men experience their vulnerability to the social pressures of homophobic blackmail; even for them, however, that is only one path of control, complementary to public sanctions through the institutions described by Foucault and others as defining and regulating the amorphous territory of "the sexual".' (Eve Kosofsky Sedgwick, *Between Men* (New York: Columbia University Press, 1985), p. 89).

[54] Review of *Gentlemen Don't Eat Poets* by Jack Matthews for the *Los Angeles Times*, 14 March 1997. Available on-line at *http://articles.latimes.com/1997-03-14/entertainment/ca-37967_1_sir-hugo-coal* (accessed 14 July 2009).

[55] Interview with Suzie Mackenzie, *Guardian*, 3 September 2005. Available on-line at *http://www.guardian.co.uk/books/2005/sep/03/fiction.features* (accessed 14 July 2009).

[56] Linda Costanzo Cahir, *Literature into Film: Theory and Practical Approaches* (Jefferson, NC: McFarland, 2006), p. 263.

2. The Transgressive Self

1   Christine Ferguson, 'McGrath's Disease: radical pathology in Patrick McGrath's neo-Gothicism', in Glennis Byron and David Punter (eds), *Spectral Readings: Towards a Gothic Geography* (New York and Basingstoke: Macmillan, 1999), pp. 233–43 (p. 242).

2   McGrath explains the process of constructing the character of 'Spider': 'I had some experience, I'd worked in a mental hospital in Canada, and I began to read some case histories and memoirs of people who suffered from schizophrenia and so on. And at that point I knew what my character looked like, I'd spotted him shambling along on a London street, he looked like Samuel Beckett, and I said, "That's the man."' Interview with Peter Murphy, 14 October 2008. Available on-line at *http://wordpress.hotpress.com/petermurphy/2008/10/14/patrick-mcgrath-confessions-of-a-dangerous-mind/* (accessed 29 May 2009). In the novel, the adult 'Spider' describes himself as 'a shuffling, spidery figure in a worn-out suit' (p. 10).

3   Scott Brewster, 'Seeing things: Gothic and the madness of interpretation', in David Punter (ed.), *A Companion to the Gothic* (Oxford: Blackwell, 2000), pp. 280–92 (p. 281).

4   Sander L. Gilman, *Disease and Representation: Images of Illness from Madness to Aids* (Ithaca and London: Cornell University Press, 1988), p. 13.

5   Michel Foucault, *Madness and Civilization: A History of Insanity in the Age of Reason*, trans. Richard Howard (London: Tavistock, 1967), p. 16.

6   Linda Hutcheon, *A Theory of Parody: The Teachings of Twentieth-Century Art Forms* (London: Methuen, 1985), p. 6.

7   Address to the Annual Meeting of the Royal College of Psychiatrists, 10 July 2001: available on-line at *http://pb.rcpsych.org/cgi/content/full/26/4/140* (accessed 9 August 2009).

8   Interview with Murphy, 14 October 2008.

9   As scholars are now beginning to recognize, even George Eliot's realism displays at times qualities of the Gothic. McGrath himself has observed, 'We even find a Gothic moment in what is considered one of the crowning glories of 19th-century realism, George Eliot's *Middlemarch*, in the character of Mr. Casaubon, black-clad, dusty scholar of the world's myths, and a figure of death, whose one small triumph is briefly to ensnare the heroine Dorothea in his moribund and ghoulish work.' ('Afterword: the new Gothic', in *Conjunctions*, 14 (Spring, 1990).) Royce Mahawatte has discussed this 'moment' in more detail in '"Beautiful lips kissing holy skulls": the counterfeit Gothic heroine in *Middlemarch*', *Gothic Studies*, 10, 2, 120–36.

10   Interview with Murphy, 14 October 2008.

11   Patrick McGrath, *Spider* (1990: Harmondsworth, Penguin, 1992), p. 13. Page numbers hereafter in the text.

12   McGrath has explained in a number of interviews that *Spider* was inspired by a collection of photographs by Bill Brandt of the East End: 'Narrow alleys at night with a lamp-post shedding a sort of dim radiance and shining off the

damp cobblestones'. (See, for example, interview in *The Times*, 28 December 2002: available on-line at *http://www.timesonline.co.uk/tol/life_and_style/article805547 .ece?token=null&offset=0&page=1* (accessed 17 May 2009).)

[13] McGrath here uses the country to which he himself was sent by his father after graduating (and where he spent some time working in a psychiatric hospital) to signify Spider's exile.

[14] See Robert Mighall, *A Geography of Victorian Gothic Fiction: Mapping History's Nightmares* (Oxford: Oxford University Press, 1999), and Julian Wolfreys, *Victorian Hauntings: Spectrality, the Uncanny and Literature* (New York and Basingstoke: Palgrave Macmillan, 2002).

[15] Ibid., pp. 43–4.

[16] Ibid., p. 66.

[17] See n.7.

[18] Lucie Armitt, 'The magical realism of the contemporary Gothic', in David Punter (ed.), *A Companion to the Gothic* (Oxford: Blackwell, 2000) pp. 305–16 (p. 311).

[19] See Barbara Creed, *The Monstrous-Feminine: Film, Feminism, Psychoanalysis* (London: Routledge, 1993).

[20] Femi Oyebode, 'Fictional narrative and psychiatry', in *Advances in Psychiatric Treatment* (2004), vol. 10, 140–5 (p. 140): available on-line at *http://apt.rcpsych.org/ cgi/reprint/10/2/140* (accessed 17 May 2009).

[21] Harold Carmel, MD, 'McGrath's fiction from the forensic asylum', *Psychiatric Services (Journal of the American Psychiatric Association)*, 49, 109–11, January 1998: available on-line at *http://psychservices.psychiatryonline.org/cgi/content/full/ 49/1/109* (accessed 9 August 2009).

[22] 'Capgras Syndrome, named for its discoverer, the French psychiatrist Jean Marie Joseph Capgras. The person's primary delusion is that a close relative or friend has been replaced by an impostor, an exact double, despite recognition of familiarity in appearance and behaviour. The patient may also see himself as his own double. Also know as delusional misidentification, illusion of doubles, illusion of negative doubles, misidentification syndrome, nonrecognition syndrome, phantom double syndrome, subjective doubles syndrome.' *(http://www. psychnet-uk.com/dsm_iv/capgras_syndrome.htm* (accessed 9 August 2009).)

[23] My translation. Falco Magali, *La Poétique néo-gothique de Patrick McGrath* (Paris: Publibook, 2007), p. 214.

[24] Interview by Nicholas Wroe, *Guardian*, 12 July 2008 .

[25] Armitt, 'Magical realism of the contemporary Gothic', p. 313.

[26] Nicholas Abraham and Maria Torok, 'The topography of reality: sketching out a metapsychology of secrets', *The Oxford Literary Review*, 12.1–2, 63–8. Cited in Armitt, 'Magical realism of the contemporary Gothic', p. 313.

[27] Armitt, 'Magical realism of the contemporary Gothic', p. 312.

[28] Robert Mighall, 'Gothic cities', in Catherine Spooner and Emma McEvoy (eds), *The Routledge Companion to Gothic* (London: Routledge, 2007), p. 35.

[29] Interview with Suzie Mackenzie, *Guardian*, 3 September 2005.

[30] See ch.1, n.2.

[31] Louis A. Sass, *Madness and Modernism: Insanity in the Light of Modern Art, Literature and Thought* (Cambridge, MA: Harvard University Press, 1992), p. 3.

[32] Foucault, *Madness and Civilization*, pp. 89, 91.

[33] Amanda Craig, 'The language of love', *Daily Telegraph*, 13 February 2006. Available on-line at *http://www.telegraph.co.uk/culture/books/3650093/The-language-of-love.html* (accessed 9 August 2009).

[34] Magali Falco suggests that one of the novel's intertexts may be Graham Greene's *The End of the Affair* (Falco, *La Poétique néo-gothique de Patrick McGrath*, p. 222.)

[35] Patrick McGrath, *Dr Haggard's Disease* (1993; Harmondsworth: Penguin Books, 1994), p. 175. Page numbers hereafter in the text.

[36] Its Scottish name is suggestive both of exile and colonialism in its echo of the 'Elgin Marbles'.

[37] 'I was accused of marrying Vincent Price and Peter Cushing but that never occurred to me either, not consciously. He was named after Cushing the great British surgeon.' E-mail correspondence with the author, 23 February 2009.

[38] The work of medically qualified Scottish novelist A. J. Cronin (1896–1981) was popular in the mid twentieth century. *The Citadel* (1937) draws on his own experience to represent the strain placed by the profession on a young doctor.

[39] Julia Kristeva, *Powers of Horror: An Essay on Abjection*, trans. Leon S. Roudiez (New York: Columbia University Press, 1982), p. 11.

[40] 'The vampire, who makes a first literary appearance in about 1800, is also biologically anomalous, being a creature distinguished by his or her inability to rot, as well as possessing a perverse and predatory sexuality. In much of Poe's best work that same theme recurs, an obsessive fascination with necrophilia, arguably the most radical of the transgressions.' (Patrick McGrath, 'Afterword: the new Gothic', in *Conjunctions*, 14, Spring 1990.)

[41] Two American novels in the 1960s, Ken Kesey's *One Flew over the Cuckoo's Nest* (1962) and Sylvia Plath's *The Bell Jar* (1963), had also ventured into representing the world of the mental hospital. The former achieved cult status with the success of the film adaptation in 1975.

[42] Patrick McGrath, *Asylum* (1996; Harmondsworth: Penguin Books, 1997), p. 95. Page numbers hereafter in the text.

[43] Interview with Wroe, 12 July 2008.

[44] Interview with Murphy, 14 October 2008.

[45] See Introduction, n.40.

[46] Interview with Tim Teeman, *The Times*, 28 December 2002. Available on-line at *http://www.timesonline.co.uk/tol/life_and_style/article805547.ece* (accessed 12 August 2009).

[47] Foucault, *Madness and Civilization*, p. 209.

[48] Ibid., p. 259.

[49] The phrase is from Philip Larkin's poem 'Annus Mirabilis', originally published in *High Windows* (London: Faber & Faber, 1967).

[50] Gilman, *Disease and Representation*, p. 89.

[51] Ibid., p. 94.

52   *The New York Times*, August 2005, available on-line at *http://movies.nytimes.com/ 2005/08/12/movies/12asyl.html?pagewanted=print* (accessed 12 August 2009); 'Spliced Wire' available on-line at *http://splicedwire.com/05reviews/ asylum.html* (accessed 12 August 2009).

3. Worlds New and Old

1   Linda Hutcheon, *A Theory of Parody: The Teachings of Twentieth-Century Art Forms* (London: Methuen, 1985), p. 6.

2   Alison Lee, *Realism and Power: Postmodern British Fiction* (London: Routledge, 1990), p. ix.

3   Taken from the customer review site for *Martha Peake* on Amazon's website at *www.amazon.co.uk* (accessed 25 July 2006).

4   Georg Lukács, *The Historical Novel*, trans. Hannah and Stanley Mitchell (London: Merlin, 1962), p. 39. Some contemporary novelists (notably Hilary Mantel in *A Place of Greater Safety* (1992) and the acclaimed *Wolf Hall* (2009)) have shown that the historical novel in this sense lives on.

5   Chris Baldick (ed.), Introduction to *Gothic Tales* (Oxford: Oxford University Press, 1992), p. xix.

6   Patrick McGrath, *Martha Peake* (2000; Harmondsworth: Penguin, 2001), p. 339. Page references hereafter in the text.

7   The use of names with popular cultural resonances is a typical McGrath strategy. 'Hawkins' evokes not only John Hawkins, famous Elizabethan sailor, and Jim Hawkins of Robert Louis Stevenson's *Treasure Island* (1883), but also the actor Jack Hawkins, the embodiment of the upright English naval officer in such films as *The Cruel Sea* (1953).

8   Linda Hutcheon, *A Poetics of Postmodernism: History, Theory, Fiction* (London: Routledge, 1988), pp. 105–6.

9   See Eve Kosofsky Sedgwick, *The Coherence of Gothic Conventions* (1980; New York and London: Methuen, 1986).

10   Umberto Eco, 'Cult movies and intertextual collage', in David Lodge (ed.), *Modern Criticism and Theory: A Reader* (London and New York: Longman, 1988), p. 453. This point is also made by Catherine Spooner in her essay 'Gothic in the twentieth century', in Catherine Spooner and Emma McEvoy (eds), *The Routledge Companion to Gothic* (London: Routledge, 2007), p. 44.

11   This is McGrath's explanation of the name: 'I liked the sound of the word. I believe it's Romanian, variation on Draco, or Dracula . . . Those associations I also liked. I visited the Devon house early in the writing of Martha Peake and seized on it, as I was hunting for good names for the book at the time'. (E-mail correspondence with the author, 18 February 2009). The 'Devon house' is Castle Drogo, a fake medieval castle built in the early twentieth century for Julius Drogo, founder of the Home and Colonial Stores. Although Drogo is also the name of Frodo Baggins's father in J. R. R. Tolkien's *The Lord of the Rings*, this seems to be a coincidence.

[12]   Peter Ackroyd, *London: The Biography* (2000: London: Vintage, 2001), p. 508.

[13]   See Jerrold E. Hogle, 'The Gothic and the "otherings" of ascendant culture: the original *Phantom of the Opera*', in Glennis Byron and David Punter (eds), *Spectral Readings: Towards a Gothic Geography* (Basingstoke: Macmillan, 1999), pp. 177–201, and Robert Miles, 'Abjection, nationalism and the Gothic', in Fred Botting (ed.), *The Gothic* (Cambridge: Brewer, 2000).

[14]   Robert Mighall, *A Geography of Victorian Gothic* (Oxford: Oxford University Press, 1999), p. xxv.

[15]   Ibid., p. 286.

[16]   Ian Duncan, *Modern Romance and Transformations of the Novel: The Gothic, Scott and Dickens* (Cambridge: Cambridge University Press, 1992), pp. 21–2.

[17]   Interview with Gilles Menegaldo, *Sources n° 5* (ed. Bernard Vincent), October 1998, 109–27 (p. 127).

[18]   Interview with Anna Battista, *Erasing Clouds*, 20 January 2004, available on-line at *http://www.erasingclouds.com/05mcgrath.html* (accessed 25 July 2006).

[19]   Patrick McGrath, *Port Mungo* (2004; London: Bloomsbury, 2005), p. 55. Page numbers hereafter in the text.

[20]   Review in the *Sunday Telegraph* by David Robson. Available on-line at *http://www.telegraph.co.uk/arts/main.jhtml?xml=/arts/2004/05/16/bomcg16.xml* (accessed 11 September 2008).

[21]   Interview for BLDG Blog, 30 July 2007. Available on-line at *http://bldgblog.blogspot.com/2007/07/possibility-of-secret-passageways.html* (accessed 3 August 2009).

[22]   McGrath, however, claims that any likeness to Virginia Woolf was not conscious. (E-mail correspondence with the author, 23 February 2009.)

[23]   Virginia Woolf, *A Room of One's Own* (1925; London: Panther, 1977), p. 35.

[24]   Virginia Woolf, *To the Lighthouse* (1927: London: Panther, 1977), p.48.

[25]   William Patrick Day, *In the Circles of Fear and Desire: A Study of Gothic Fantasy* (Chicago: University of Chicago Press, 1985), p. 64.

[26]   Magali Falco, 'The painting of the urban dreamscape in Patrick McGrath's *Port Mungo*'; available on-line at *http://sites.univ-provence.fr/e-rea/5_2/5_2_PDF/8_Falco.pdf* (accessed 11 September 2008).

[27]   Michael Bell, *Literature, Modernism and Myth* (Cambridge: Cambridge University Press, 1997), p. 226.

[28]   Andrew Smith, 'Rethinking the Gothic: what do we mean?', *Gothic Studies* (2002), 4, 1, 79–85.

[29]   Stephen Dedalus uses the phrase 'smithy of my soul' in *A Portrait of the Artist as a Young Man* (1916; Oxford: Oxford University Press, 2000), p. 213.

[30]   See McGrath's comments in his interview with Nicholas Wroe: 'The labelling as a gothic writer in his early career did become problematic, and he complains that it encouraged people not to read the books attentively because "they think they know what's going on before they start. Certainly in something like *The Grotesque*, and even in *Martha Peake*, I was being very deliberately gothic. In other books I thought I was trying to fry different fish."' Interview with Nicholas Wroe, *Guardian*, 12 July 2008.

31 Interview in *Scotland on Sunday*, 18 September 2005. Available on-line at *http://living.scotsman.com/features/Haunted-by-wraiths-of-New.2662223.jp* (accessed 25 September 2009).

32 Interview with Suzie Mackenzie, *Guardian*, 3 September 2005.

33 Todd McEwen, *Guardian*, 24 September 2005; available on-line at *http://www. guardian.co.uk/books/2005/sep/24/featuresreviews.guardianreview18* (accessed 26 September 2009).

34 Max Byrd "'Ghost Town'": Gothic Gotham', *New York Times*, 4 September 2005; available on-line at *http://www.nytimes.com/2005/09/04/books/review/ 04BYRD.html?_r=1* (accessed 26 September 2009).

35 "'We all have dreaming minds'", *Patrick McGrath and Louise Welsh on Gothic Nightmares', Tate Etc.*, Spring 2006. Available on-line at *http://www.tate.org.uk/ tateetc/issue6/gothicnightmares.htm* (accessed 27 September 2009).

36 Peter Buse and Andrew Stott, *Ghosts: Deconstruction, Psychoanalysis and History* (Basingstoke: Palgrave Macmillan, 1999), p. 10.

37 Patrick McGrath, *Ghost Town: Tales of Manhattan Then and Now* (London: Bloomsbury, 2005), p. 2. Page numbers hereafter in the text.

38 As Buse and Stott point out, this is a term favoured by Derrida. The Derridean revenant is 'the thing that returns' and which 'comes to represent a mobilization of familiar Derridean concepts such as trace, iteration and the deferral of presence.' (Buse and Stott, *Ghosts*, p. 10.)

39 Some reviewers likened its narrative style to that of several nineteenth-century authors. Peter McCarty, in the *Independent*, for example, wrote 'McGrath recreates a world of scheming scriveners, of riches amassed and of tragedies precipitated by ironclad propriety. There are elements of Dickens, James and Melville here, but these influences meld into an inimitable tale.' Peter Carty, Review of *Ghost Town* in the *Independent*, 15 September 2005; available on-line at *http://www.independent.co.uk/arts-entertainment/books/reviews/ghost-town-by- patrick-mcgrath-506842.html* (accessed 26 September 2009).

40 Interview with Suzie Mackenzie, *Guardian*, 3 September 2005.

41 John Ashcroft was the US Attorney General at the time of the attack. He was responsible for the curtailing of civil liberties in the name of the 'War on Terror', enshrined in the Patriot Act, which George W. Bush signed into law on 26 October 2001.

42 See Jerrold E. Hogle, *The Undergrounds of The Phantom of the Opera: Sublimation and the Gothic in Leroux's Novel and its Progeny* (New York and Basingstoke: Palgrave Macmillan, 2002), for a detailed analysis of the process of cultural abjection.

4. Afterword

1 E-mail correspondence with the author, 18 February 2009.

2 Adam Mars Jones, Review of *Trauma*, *Observer*, 20 July 2008. Available on-line at *http://www.guardian.co.uk/books/2008/jul/20/fiction3* (accessed 2 February 2009).

3   Interview with Peter Murphy, October 2008.
4   Ed King, Review of *Trauma*, 18 July 2008, *Daily Telegraph*. Available on-line at
     *http://www.telegraph.co.uk/culture/books/fictionreviews/3556392/Trauma-the-
     mind-doctors-mind.html* (accessed 3 September 2009).
5   Adam Mars Jones, Review of *Trauma*, *Observer*, 20 July 2008.
6   Interview with Nicholas Wroe, *Guardian*, 12 July 2008.
7   Anne Williams, *Art of Darkness: A Poetics of Gothic* (Chicago: University of Chicago
     Press, 1995), p. 99.

Select Bibliography

൙൚

Works by Patrick McGrath

Fiction

Blood and Water (1988; Harmondsworth: Penguin, 1989).

The Grotesque (1989; Harmondsworth: Penguin, 1990).

Spider (1990; Harmondsworth: Penguin, 1992).

'Cleave the Vampire or a Gothic Pastorale', in Michelle Slung, *I Shudder at your Touch* (New York: New American Library, 1991); retitled 'Not Cricket' in the British edition in the same year (Harmondsworth: Penguin, 1991), pp. 117–30.

Dr Haggard's Disease (1993; Harmondsworth: Penguin, 1994).

Asylum (1996; Harmondsworth: Penguin, 1997).

Martha Peake: A Novel of the Revolution (2000; Harmondsworth: Penguin, 2001).

Port Mungo (2004; London: Bloomsbury, 2005).

Ghost Town: Tales of Manhattan Then and Now (London: Bloomsbury, 2005).

Edited Collections

(With Bradford Morrow), *The New Gothic: A Collection of Contemporary Gothic Fiction* (New York: Random House, 1991).

Articles and Essays

'Afterword: the new Gothic', in *Conjunctions*, 14, Spring 1990. Available on-line at *http://www.conjunctions.com/archives/c14-pm.htm* (accessed 5 July 2009).

'Transgression and Decay', in Cristoph Grunenberg (ed.), *Gothic: Transmutations of Horror in Late Twentieth-Century Art* (Cambridge, MA: MIT Press, 1997), pp. 158–3. (The pagination runs backwards in this volume.)

Critical Sources: Patrick McGrath

Falco, Magali, *La Poétique néo-gothique de Patrick McGrath* (Paris: Publibook, 2007).

Falco, Magali, 'The painting of the urban dreamscape in Patrick McGrath's *Port Mungo*'. Available on-line at *http://sites.univ-provence.fr/e-rea/5_2/5_2_PDF/8_Falco.pdf* (accessed 11 September 2008).

Ferguson, Christine, 'McGrath's disease: radical pathology in Patrick McGrath's neo-Gothicism', in Glennis Byron and David Punter (eds), *Spectral Readings: Towards a Gothic Geography* (New York and Basingstoke: Palgrave Macmillan, 1999), pp. 233–43.

Green, Colin, 'Back to school: a note on Patrick McGrath's "Ambrose Syme"', in *Peake Studies*, 1, 4 (Summer 1990), 5–8.

Oyebode, Femi, 'Fictional narrative and psychiatry', in *Advances in Psychiatric Treatment* (2004), vol. 10, 140–5. Available on-line at *http://apt.rcpsych.org/cgi/reprint/10/2/140* (accessed 17 May 2009).

Critical Sources: The Gothic

Aguirre, Manuel, 'Narrative structure, liminality, self-similarity: the case of Gothic fiction', in Isabel Soto (ed.), *A Place that is Not a Place: Essays in Liminality and Text* (Madrid: Gateway Press, 2000), pp. 134–51.

Armitt, Lucie, 'The magical realism of the contemporary Gothic', in David Punter (ed.), *A Companion to the Gothic* (Oxford: Blackwell, 2000), pp. 305–16.

Baldick, Chris (ed.), Introduction to *Gothic Tales* (Oxford: Oxford University Press, 1992).

Baldick, Chris and Robert Mighall, 'Gothic criticism', in David Punter (ed.), *A Companion to the Gothic* (Oxford: Blackwell, 2000).

Botting, Fred (ed.), *The Gothic* (Cambridge: Brewer, 2001).

Brewster, Scott, 'Seeing things: Gothic and the madness of interpretation', in David Punter (ed.), *A Companion to the Gothic* (Oxford: Blackwell, 2000), pp. 280–92.

Buse, Peter and Andrew Stott, *Ghosts: Deconstruction, Psychoanalysis and History* (New York and Basingstoke: Palgrave Macmillan, 1999).

Castle, Terry, *The Female Thermometer: Eighteenth Century Culture and the Invention of the Uncanny* (Oxford: Oxford University Press, 1995).

Creed, Barbara, *The Monstrous-Feminine: Film, Feminism, Psychoanalysis* (London: Routledge, 1993).

Davenport-Hines, Richard, *Gothic: 400 Years of Excess, Horror, Evil and Ruin* (London: Fourth Estate, 1998).

Day, William Patrick, *In the Circles of Fear and Desire: A Study of Gothic Fantasy* (Chicago: University of Chicago Press, 1985).

Duncan, Ian, *Modern Romance and Transformations of the Novel: The Gothic, Scott and Dickens* (Cambridge: Cambridge University Press, 1992).

Hendershot, Cyndy, *The Animal Within: Masculinity and the Gothic* (Ann Arbor: University of Michigan Press, 1998).

Hogle, Jerrold E., 'The Gothic and the "otherings" of ascendant culture: the original *Phantom of the Opera*', in Glennis Byron and David Punter (eds), *Spectral Readings: Towards a Gothic Geography* (Basingstoke: Macmillan, 1999), pp. 177–201.

Hogle, Jerrold E., 'The Gothic at the turn of the century: our culture of simulation and the return of the body', in Fred Botting (ed.), *The Gothic* (London: Brewer, 2000).

Hogle, Jerrold E., *The Undergrounds of The Phantom of the Opera: Sublimation and the Gothic in Leroux's Novel and its Progeny* (New York and Basingstoke: Palgrave Macmillan, 2002).

Horner, Avril and Sue Zlosnik, *Gothic and the Comic Turn* (New York and Basingstoke: Palgrave Macmillan, 2005).

Hurley, Kelly, *The Gothic Body: Sexuality, Materialism, and Degeneration at the Fin de Siècle* (Cambridge: Cambridge University Press, 1996).

Lévy, Maurice, '"Gothic" and the critical idiom', in Allan Lloyd-Smith and Victor Sage (eds), *Gothick Origins and Innovations* (Amsterdam: Rodopi Press, 1994), pp. 1–15.

Mason, Diane, "'A very devil with the men'": the pathology and iconography of the erotic consumptive and the attractive masturbator', in *Gothic Studies*, 2, 2 (August 2000) 205–17.

Mighall, Robert, "'A pestilence which walketh in darkness'": diagnosing the Victorian vampire', in Glennis Byron and David Punter (eds), *Spectral Readings: Towards a Gothic Geography* (Basingstoke: Macmillan Press, 1999).

Mighall, Robert, *A Geography of Victorian Gothic Fiction: Mapping History's Nightmares* (Oxford: Oxford University Press, 1999).

Miles, Robert, *Gothic Writing 1750–1820*, 2nd edition (Manchester: Manchester University Press, 2002).

Miles, Robert, 'Abjection, nationalism and the Gothic', in Fred Botting (ed.), *The Gothic* (Cambridge: Brewer, 2000).

Ng, Andrew Hock-Soon, *Dimensions of Monstrosity in Contemporary Fiction* (New York and Basingstoke: Palgrave Macmillan, 2004).

Punter, David, *The Literature of Terror, Vol. 2 The Modern Gothic*, 2nd edition (London: Longman, 1996).

Royle, Nicholas, *The Uncanny* (Manchester: Manchester University Press, 2003).

Sage, Victor, *Horror Fiction in the Protestant Tradition* (New York and Basingstoke: Palgrave Macmillan, 1988).

Sedgwick, Eve Kosofsky, *The Coherence of Gothic Conventions* (1980; New York and London: Methuen, 1986).

Smith, Allan Lloyd, 'Postmodernism/Gothicism', in Victor Sage and Allan Lloyd Smith (eds), *Modern Gothic: A Reader* (Manchester: University Press, 1996).

Smith, Andrew, *Gothic Literature* (Edinburgh: Edinburgh University Press, 2007).

Smith, Andrew, 'Rethinking the Gothic: what do we mean?', *Gothic Studies* (2002) 4, 1, 79–85.

Warwick, Alexandra, 'Victorian Gothic', in Catherine Spooner and Emma McEvoy, *The Routledge Companion to the Gothic* (Oxford and New York: Routledge, 2007).

Williams, Anne, *Art of Darkness: A Poetics of Gothic* (Chicago: University of Chicago Press, 1995).

Williamson, Milly, *The Lure of the Vampire: Gender, Fiction and Fandom from Bram Stoker to Buffy* (London: Wallflower Press, 2005).

Wolfreys, Julian, *Victorian Hauntings: Spectrality, the Uncanny and Literature* (New York and Basingstoke: Palgrave Macmillan, 2002).

Wolfreys, Julian, 'Preface', in Ruth Robbins and Julian Wolfreys (eds), *Victorian Gothic: Literary and Cultural Manifestations in the Nineteenth Century* (New York and Basingstoke: Palgrave Macmillan, 2000), pp. i–xi.

Other Critical and Historical Sources

Ackroyd, Peter, *London: The Biography* (2000: London: Vintage, 2001).

Bakhtin, Mikhail, *The Dialogic Imagination: Four Essays*, ed. Michael Holquist, trans. Caryl Emerson and Michael Holquist (Austin: University of Texas Press, 1981).

Bell, Michael, *Literature, Modernism and Myth* (Cambridge: Cambridge University Press, 1997).

Cahir , Linda Costanzo, *Literature into Film: Theory and Practical Approaches* (Jefferson, NC: McFarland, 2006).

Dentith, Simon, *Parody* (London: Routledge, 2000).

Eco, Umberto, 'Postmodernism, irony and the enjoyable', in Peter Brooker, *Modernism/Postmodernism* (Harlow: Longman, 1992).

Eco, Umberto, 'Cult movies and intertextual collage', in David Lodge (ed.), *Modern Criticism and Theory: A Reader* (London and New York: Longman, 1988).

Foucault, Michel, *Madness and Civilization: A History of Insanity in the Age of Reason*, trans. Richard Howard (London: Tavistock, 1967).

Freud, Sigmund, 'The Uncanny' (1919), in *Sigmund Freud: The Penguin Freud Library* (London: Penguin Books, 1985), vol. 14, 'Art and Literature', p. 345.

Gilman, Sander L., *Disease and Representation: Images of Illness from Madness to Aids* (Ithaca and London: Cornell University Press, 1988).

Hutcheon, Linda, *A Theory of Parody: The Teachings of Twentieth-Century Art Forms* (London: Methuen, 1985).

Hutcheon, Linda, *A Poetics of Postmodernism: History, Theory, Fiction* (London: Routledge, 1988).

Kayser, Wolfgang, *The Grotesque in Art and Literature*, trans. Ulrich Weisstein (Bloomington: Indiana University Press, 1957).

Kristeva, Julia, *Powers of Horror: An Essay on Abjection*, trans. Leon S. Roudiez (New York: Columbia University Press, 1982).

Lee, Alison, *Realism and Power: Postmodern British Fiction* (London: Routledge, 1990).

Lukács, Georg, *The Historical Novel*, trans. Hannah and Stanley Mitchell (London: Merlin, 1962).

Rose, Margaret, *Parody: Ancient, Modern and Post-Modern* (Cambridge: Cambridge University Press, 1993).

Sass, Louis A., *Madness and Modernism: Insanity in the Light of Modern Art, Literature and Thought* (Cambridge, MA: Harvard University Press, 1992).

Sedgwick, Eve Kosofsky, *Between Men* (New York: Columbia University Press, 1985).

White, Allon and Peter Stallybrass, *The Politics and Poetics of Transgression* (Ithaca: Cornell University Press, 1986).

Interviews with Patrick McGrath

Battista, Anna, *Erasing Clouds*, 20 January 2004, at *http://www.erasingclouds.com/05mcgrath.html* (accessed 25 July 2006).

BLDG Blog at *http://bldgblog.blogspot.com/2007/07/possibility-of-secret-passageways.html* (accessed 3 August 2009).

Falco, Magali, *A Collection of Interviews with Patrick McGrath* (Paris: Éditions Publibook, 2007).

Mackenzie, Suzie, *Guardian*, 3 September 2005, at *http://www.guardian.co.uk/books/2005/sep/03/fiction.features* (accessed 14 July 2009).

Menegaldo, Gilles, *Sources n° 5* (ed. Bernard Vincent), October 1998, 109–27.

Murphy, Peter, 14 October 2008, at *http://wordpress.hotpress.com/petermurphy/2008/10/14/patrick-mcgrath-confessions-of-a-dangerous-mind/* (accessed 29 May 2009).

Scotland on Sunday, 18 September 2005, at *http://living.scotsman.com/features/Haunted-by-wraiths-of-New.2662223.jp* (accessed 7 September 2009).

Teeman, Tim, *The Times*, 28 December 2002, at *http://www.timesonline.co.uk/tol/life_and_style/article805547.ece* (accessed 29 May 2009).

Wroe, Nicholas, *Guardian*, 12 July 2008, at *http://www.guardian.co.uk/books/2008/jul/12/saturdayreviewsfeatres.guardianreview19* (accessed 26 February 2009).

Other Web Sources

McGrath, Patrick, 'Address to the Annual Meeting of the Royal College of Psychiatrists', 10 July 2001 (accessed on-line at *http://pb.rcpsych.org/cgi/content/full/26/4/140* 9 August 2009).

McGrath, Patrick and Louise Welsh, 'We all have dreaming minds', *Tate Etc.*, *Spring 2006, at http://www.tate.org.uk/tateetc/issue6/gothicnightmares.htm* (accessed 27 September 2009). *http://www.psychnet-uk.com/dsm_iv/ capgras_syndrome.htm* (accessed 9 August 2009).

Reviews

Byrd, Max, '"Ghost Town": Gothic Gotham', *The New York Times*, 4 September 2005, at *http://www.nytimes.com/ 2005/09/04/books/ review/04BYRD.html?_r=1* (accessed 26 September 2009).

Carmel, Harold, 'McGrath's fiction from the forensic asylum', *Psychiatric Services (Journal of the American Psychiatric Association)*, 49 (January 1998), 109–11. Available on-line at http://psychservices.psychiatryonline.org/ cgi/content/full/49/1/109 (accessed 9 August 2009).

Carty, Peter, Review of *Ghost Town*, *Independent*, 15 September 2005, at *http://www.independent.co.uk/arts-entertainment/books/reviews/ghost-town-by-patrick-mcgrath-506842.html* (accessed 26 September 2009).

Hensher, Philip, Review of *Martha Peake*, *Observer*, 20 August 2000, at *http://www.guardian.co.uk/books/2000/aug/20/fiction.reviews3* (accessed 26 February 2009).

King, Ed, Review of *Trauma*, *Telegraph*, 18 July 2008, at *http://www. telegraph.co.uk/ culture/books/fictionreviews/3556392/Trauma-the-mind-doctors-mind.html* (accessed 3 September 2009).

McEwen, Todd, Review of *Ghost Town*, *Guardian*, 24 September 2005, at *http://www.guardian.co.uk/books/2005/sep/24/featuresreviews.guardianreview 18* (accessed 26 September 2009).

Mars-Jones, Adam, Review of *Trauma*, *Observer*, 20 July 2008, at *http:// www. guardian.co.uk/books/2008/jul/20/fiction3* (accessed 2 February 2009).

Robson, David, Review of *Port Mungo*, *Sunday Telegraph*, 18 May 2004, at *http://www.telegraph.co.uk/arts/main.jhtml?xml=/arts/2004/05/16/bomc g16.xml* (accessed 11 September 2008).

Film Reviews

Craig, Amanda, 'The language of love', *Telegraph*, 13 February 2006, at *http://www.telegraph.co.uk/culture/books/3650093/The-language-of-love.html* (accessed 9 August 2009).

Dargis, Manohla, Review of *Asylum*, *The New York Times*, August 2005, at *http://movies.nytimes.com/2005/08/12/movies/12asyl.html?pagewanted= print* (accessed 12 August 2008).

Matthews, Jack, Review of *Gentlemen Don't Eat Poets*, *Los Angeles Times*, 14 March 1997, at *http://articles.latimes.com/1997-03-14/entertainment/ ca-37967_1_sir-hugo-coal* (accessed 14 July 2009).

Review of *Asylum*, 'Spliced Wire', at *http://splicedwire.com/05reviews/asylum. html* (accessed 12 August 2008).

Index

ஐ෦